# LIVING IN **PEACE** WHILE LIVING IN **PIECES**

*A Memoir*

**Michael Washington**

# LIVING IN PEACE WHILE LIVING IN PIECES

© *2021 by Michael Washington. All rights reserved.*

*No part of this book may be reproduced or transmitted in any form or by any means, electronic or mechanical, including photocopying, recording, or by any information storage and retrieval system, without permission in writing from the copyright owner.*

Printed in United States of America

This book is printed on acid-freepaper.

# CONTENTS

ACKNOWLEDGEMENTS ........................................................ 5
ENDORSEMENT ..................................................................... 6
PREFACE .................................................................................. 8
INTRODUCTION ................................................................... 10

**Chapter 1**
    A Tribute to My Peace ...................................................... 1

**Chapter 2**
    The Essence of Living in Peace ....................................... 4

**Chapter 3**
    The Genesis of My Peace ............................................... 13

**Chapter 4**
    Emergence of My Peace and Pieces ............................ 18

**Chapter 5**
    Boundaries of Peace and Pieces .................................. 27

**Chapter 6**
    Subsidiary of Peace ....................................................... 33

**Chapter 7**
    Managing the Peace and Pieces ................................... 39

**Chapter 8**
    Marriage with Peace and Pieces .................................. 61

**Chapter 9**
    Unobstructed Peace ....................................................... 66

**Chapter 10**

    Interrupted Peace ............................................................ 75

**Chapter 11**

    The Deep Pit of My Pieces ............................................ 83

**Chapter 12**

    Deep Pit of Pieces — Part II

    (My Wife's Perspective) ............................................. 103

**Chapter 13**

    Securing the Peace within Me ................................... 121

**Chapter 14**

    Pieces Coming Together ............................................. 138

**Chapter 15**

    The Ultimate Guardian of My Peace ....................... 147

**Chapter 16**

    Anchored in Peace ....................................................... 158

# ACKNOWLEDGEMENTS

It is my greatest pleasure to acknowledge the many people, family and friends, who have contributed to the success in accomplishing the production of my first book. I thank my wife, Glenda, for sharing the journey of developing this book with me. I also thank her for allowing me to share her story while expanding the understanding of what a wife and partner in life must encounter dealing with an addicted spouse. I thank our three daughters, Sharmaine, Porsha, and Michelle for their continued love and appreciation. I thank my father and mother for their loving efforts to raise a family of seven children (Jimmie, Robert, Alice, Sammie Jr., Shirley, and Stephanie) and for being the beacon for us to follow.

I would also like to acknowledge those who contributed so much to the accuracy of portions of the book, particularly my sister Alice Young, as well as a friend for many years, Michael Winston. They helped me recall events that occurred many years ago when I lived in St. Louis. Alice and Mike's input were invaluable to me.

I would especially like to thank Mark Bradley, a good friend, who's persistent encouragement helped me to even begin this journey of authorship. Quite frankly, my appreciation extends well beyond those I have mentioned because my story could not have been told if I had not engaged with the hundreds of friends, associates, and family members who have contributed to my life's journey.

# ENDORSEMENT

Thanks for sharing with the world, the pieces that defined your person, your life journey, and your life. I have read many books in life, Mike. But, apart from the Bible, I feel bold to say that your book is one of those that have impacted me the most. I think it's not just the content of the story, but the moral force, the sincerity of heart, and the simplicity of the rendition that gave the 'story' the authority and transformational power. It has a unique capacity to touch and impact lives.

Your story is powerful, not only because yours was hands-on experience, but your wife's contribution provided a window for readers to view the agony of spouses, mothers, and near-relatives who have to attend to substance abusers. I want to thank you and your wife particularly for this. Again, her testimony was powerful, and many spouses and mothers could identify easily with that flow of her narrative. Her words, were spirit and life. She also brought the stamp of faith, and divine providence into the entire experience, because in the final analysis, it was God that brought the victory to you as a family. When you said" My wife....has played a huge role in solidifying our marriage for all these years and is always the one to offer the practical solutions to problems we face....a solid rock of greatness and strength", you are by this validating what every man who has gone through the twists and turns of life with a supporting wife by their side can identify with, and God's eternal declaration, in that " It is not good for man to be alone". Thank God for faithful wives and mothers.

Although there are many nuggets of wisdom contained in your story. I want to just make reference three because they are so essential to success in the marketplace and indeed necessary for life convergence:

Self-inflicted barriers: We have within each of us, the capacity for good and evil. Yes, a lot of things are thrown at us on our life journey, but it is the thoughts we internalize, the choices we make, and actions (or inactions) we willingly adopt, that determine whether we will reach our goal or not. Coming to terms with self is not an easy enterprise. This is where Christian faith is so powerful - the idea that we inherit an Adamic nature that has to be put to death, and a new man made possible through the substitutionary death of Christ, is the ultimate solution to the human predicament.

Attitude determines altitude: Through a positive attitude, a denial arising from racial prejudices was eventually reversed at your work place; the IT saboteurs made 180 degrees turnaround; the mother-in-law eventually gave her approval...etc. This theme ran through the story. We may not have control over things thrown at us, but we have control over "how" we react - and since this is within our control, that puts us at the driving seat of our lives.

Unconditional love: you said "the lessons learned have elevated my ability to be a better person and increased my ability to embody unconditional love, enabling me to work in peace". This statement encapsulates the reason for our existence. When we eventually stand before our maker, this might well be the most important parameter for our performance evaluation. Have you learned to love? That is the ultimate question we all must answer.

I congratulate you for coming to this essential conclusion with your life story, and I pray that the Lord who healed your mother of breast cancer; delivered you from the pit of substance abuse; enabled you to finish strong in your career and write this book; the same Lord will uphold you and your wonderful family for the rest of your days.

Bunmi Obembe

# PREFACE

OVER THE PAST TWENTY YEARS, I have shared many of my life's experiences and philosophical views with others. When speaking candidly about matters close to my heart, many people suggested I write a book, an idea that had never crossed my mind. After hearing the same over and over, I summoned the resolve to write my first book. Living in Peace While Living in Pieces informs the reader about my temperament through conscientious reflections that uncover some of the darkest and brightest moments of my life journey. It reveals problematic addictions and mistakes I made during my life and how I managed to recover through help from others. It captures my personal belief system and the beginnings of my early childhood's invisible wounds, and it provides an acknowledgment of productive endeavors from my life lessons. Through good and bad circumstances, I have been able to maintain a peaceful life.

I have traveled extensively for business and pleasure throughout the United States and have met people from many backgrounds. I have also traveled abroad, experiencing the different cultures in many places. Howbeit briefly, I have gained an appreciation of how various people think and live.

Although my formal education involved the sciences in geology and meteorology, my work history includes an acquired acumen concerning diverse human resource skills in performance management, public relations, workforce planning, community affairs, facilitation, and equal employment programs. In particular, I have been honored with several awards in recognition of consistent exemplary accomplishments, facilitating communications between departments, agencies, and employees. I have had tremendous success designing training programs that improved performance and productivity in the work environment and created workshops and drills to ensure employees could properly apply concepts. In my job, I was recognized as a subject matter expert on many diversity issues while traveling to multiple offices to educate employees on related issues. At 50 years old, I was at the height of my career, doing my dream job in a place that suited me well. My children were grown and all three had graduated college. My wife and I seemed solid in our twenty odd year marriage. At this point, I had worked for the federal government for twenty plus years traveling across this country and had been involved with several organizations. I was in what some would consider a high paid position as a Meteorologist. I had utilized impressive diplomatic and leadership skills throughout my professional career. In the early 90s, I was an Observations Program manager where I helped transition in new observing weather programs. I had also served as a Radar Program manager where I helped the agency successfully install Dopplar Radar systems throughout our eastern region. I had served as Warning Coordination Meteorologist in a local forecast office where I championed several new technologies. I had taught meteorology as an adjunct professor. I had served on several committees and received numerous certificates and awards. I had also served as one of a local chapter's Blacks in Government president where I led and developed the chapter's first strategic planning effort. I was also an ordained deacon within a nationwide church organization. I knew a lot of people everywhere. Life was good, or so it seemed. Imagine my surprise when I realized, I finally realized, I had a serious problem. I succumbed to a drug addiction but overcame. I'll elaborate on this aspect of my life in a later chapter. My personal life experiences coupled with the understanding and knowledge I gained from those endeavors have equipped me with a keen sense of human behavior. At this stage in my life, I believe I have positioned myself to discuss many of my philosophical views about peaceful living while providing the essence of how I have lived in peace.

# INTRODUCTION

I have experienced amazing twist and turns in my life and I've learned to be transparent with my words and deeds. The most important and the one common thread throughout this my book is the peace I have maintained because of my faith in God. My belief in God is my foundation and a fundamental choice of how I try to live out my life. I have attempted to live for Christ, not in a perfect way, I must admit, but in one that honors and trusts God's word that he will make a way for me to live with his dignity. I believe through his grace, God generously provides the salvation I so desperately need.

We live in a deceitful world filled with evil, malevolence and malicious malcontent. As with many facets of life, I believe Christians will always live in pieces, experiencing adversities, sufferings, and hardships. But I have a hope, and that hope is in Christ Jesus, who shed his blood and died for all mankind. But Jesus was resurrected, and his spirit now lives within me. This life is short, but all believers who accept Christ, as Lord and savior, have the faith that he lives and the confidence of eternal life. I am a person of faith in the body of believers and have not always made decisions that please God, but my trials have always been a resultant for my good. But for the grace of God, one of my experiences could have been yours or one of your loved ones.

There is currently a renewed focus on opioids and the looming drug crisis of 2017. Suicides are being committed at more alarming rates now than ever before. People are losing their ability to cope which is one of the reasons why people turn to drugs. Their circumstances may inform them that suicide is a better option than living because they see no escape from the complexities of their immediate or current circumstance. In some cases, they may have difficulty navigating through the emptiness inside but there is always hope.

Addicts should not be viewed as the worst people in the world and they are not the greatest sinners. Addicts are people, often in pain, using poor judgement for one reason or another. This is likely a description that could fit quite a few people. Like many people in pain, instead of seeking positive support, we tend to turn to something that gives momentary relief but can have unexpected prolonged repercussions. Like the examples put before us in the Word of God, He uses ordinary, flawed people to touch the lives of other ordinary flawed people. I am such an example. May God bless you as you read my story. I hope you see Him, His faithfulness and all that He is capable of and always give Him the glory, honor, and praise.

# CHAPTER 1

## A Tribute to My Peace

My tribute to peace was not conceived or recognized until I began to recall many of my life experiences, good and bad. It involved a great deal of reflection and purpose. I gave great consideration to what I would talk about and how my book would benefit those inclined to read it. I also considered what would make Living in Peace While Living in Pieces different and considered the fact that every one of us must live in pieces, but many of us live out our lives without peace or contentment. I began to consciously probe my mind about the choices I made in life that led to consequential failures, problematic drug use, and long-term hemorrhaging effects to my state of mind. As I pondered and further examined my personal behavior over the past years, I considered the resilience from my physical and psychological battle scars, which are essentially the pieces of my life. I instinctively knew I was no different from anyone else because we all face the weight of life's exigencies. I reflected on the bad choices I had made in the past and the personal conflicts I encountered during my life, and wondered how I made it this far in life despite the grief and hardships. I have a marriage that has lasted more than forty years. I have three wonderful daughters who have grown to be great stewards of productive lives. I have enjoyed a long and successful career that has provided my family and me some material comforts, and I have managed to consistently have contentment during my life's journey. I asked myself, how was I able to maintain contentment with all of my life's failures, disappointments, psychological wounds, and addictions?

It took a little reflection, but here's what I determined. My peace began during my childhood when I accepted Jesus Christ as my personal savior. It is from His grace and through His goodness that my mind is seldom clouded with resentment. Through His unconditional love, He has shown me how to choose love over hate, creating within me an unyielding level of peace in my life. It was from this vantage where I began to assimilate my life's personal experiences and considered the book's title about living in peace. As these thoughts raced through my mind, I felt the need to discuss my life's journey while sharing my views on peaceful living. During my life, I have made many bad choices that have consequentially affected me and impacted lives of others. My life's journey has also included a remarkable resilience from those poor choices that I consider to be building blocks of my character.

When I began to write Living in Peace While Living in Pieces, the title had not been etched into my mind, but I knew it would be about peace because I have lived in peace most of my life. After I had written a portion of the manuscript, a virus entered my computer, which nearly destroyed my hard drive, and I lost the entire document without having a backup file. After the virus was removed, the document still could not be found. At this point, I had devoted precious time, and all seemed to have been in vain. I began to think about how all the work of my initial efforts had been lost, never to be recaptured. This undeniable happenstance was very discouraging and nearly led to my giving up the idea. In a brief moment, I was temporarily living in pieces, something I could never avoid. I fought the temptation to quit and began to start over. As I began to write and recapture my initial thoughts, to my astonishment, my ideas seemed to be more coherent and the content more intriguing than my first attempt. I then realized the loss of the first document was actually not in vain, as I initially thought, but necessary.

Through this book, I intend to expose part of my life's

journey by uncovering the good and bad with a humble desire to inspire others to reach for their comfort of peace. My views are mine alone and should not be seen as an expert take on peace; they are simply my opinion derived from observations and personal experiences. Through my story, I want you to personally capture the essence of living in peace while treading the unfortunate pieces of your life.

My ability to maintain a peaceful life, even while enduring many afflictions, has been accomplished by a simple desire to love and to forgive. I am reminded of a quote by William Shakespeare, who stated many years ago, "Love all, trust a few, and do wrong to none." These few words still have profound meaning that, to me, provokes consequential thought. Loving everyone, regardless of your disposition or feelings, can be freeing and allows you to readily forgive those who have done you wrong. By trusting only a few, you protect yourself from being vulnerable to all types of misgivings by those who would potentially cause you harm or from scams that persist in the world. And by doing no wrong to anyone, you show a commitment to your moral or spiritual values, which promotes good will and civility. In my opinion, these are important principles to live by and can have a significant impact on your life. But if you want consistent peace in your life, the challenge is to think positive thoughts, overcome fear with love, and develop patience. If you can accomplish these three things, you are on your way to enjoying a peaceful life while experiencing the unequivocal impacts of living in pieces.

# CHAPTER 2
## The Essence of Living in Peace

I BELIEVE THE FOUNDATION OF PEACE is having a positive outlook on life. In other words, no matter what you are going through in life, good or bad, a positive attitude will help to support a peaceful state of mind. Thinking positive is so important because it counteracts the negative gravitational pull in response to how you feel at any given moment in time. All of our thoughts are derived and generated from a state of mind, and our actions and behaviors will follow, demonstrating the true nature or condition of a mind-set. Therefore, positive thinking cannot be understated. To live in peace also requires a resolve to be humble and unselfish. The primary distinguishing features of peaceful living are being able to freely love, having an ability to forgive, and having a willingness to make sacrifices. These three laudable attributes of a mind-set, alone, can yield tremendous peace in your life. On the other hand, consistently having little or no peace in your life will manifest a temperament of fear, hatred, and doubt. This temperament will normally demonstrate as having a lack of emotional control, not being able to forgive trespasses, and taking things too personally. However, all of the above emanates from a thinking pattern or emotional construct that will ultimately reveal, what I have coined, a person's peace quotient. Although a mathematical term, your peace quotient in this context can be determined by an overall thinking pattern that demonstrates the preponderance of either negative or positive thinking. In my view, enjoying a peaceful life is not simply the ebbs and flow of a conscious state of mind but a prevailing product of clear, rational thinking. Yes, it is rational to think positive.

I believe we all consciously or subconsciously want to live in peace, but many do not achieve this attainable but elusive fulfillment. Living in peace is a mental state of tranquility that engenders harmony and quietly endures the hard knocks of life. The pieces, according to my determination, are the bad and ugly tremors of life that no one wants but which are natural occurrences and inevitable parts of life's journey. Life is short, but the journey seems long. Unfortunately, many of us spend our entire lives in pieces, never enjoying the peace of mind we all desire and deserve. Enjoying consistent peace while enduring the agonizing pieces can have long-term consequences. The consequences of peace will allow you to experience the satisfaction of perpetual contentment, but the consequences of pieces without peace can result in discontentment or permanent despair in some cases.

Everyone would agree that life is a precious commodity and should be cherished and celebrated. However, the road is tough, clouded by fear, embroiled with turmoil, and filled with troubles. Simply by your existence, you will, consequentially, encounter all kinds of mischiefs, divisions, and storms of discontent. These are only a few problematic skirmishes of life that we must combat, many of which occur conspicuously throughout our lives and sometimes through no fault of our own. I am a realist and tend to see things as they are, and I have truly accepted the fact that we, as human beings, are imperfect creatures.

The very important and even the mundane things we do in life hinge on whether or not we have consistent peace. For instance, living day to day attending to routine affairs at home, on the job, or even shopping to maintain a standard of living can be gratifying in the moment. Although we may not give it much conscious thought, peace can be obtained by hanging out with friends, attending group functions, or simply spending time at home with family, which are moments in time we should cherish. Celebrating birthdays, graduations, anniversaries, and important accomplishments and observing holidays all contribute to enjoying a peaceful life.

When we think of the idea of excitement in our lives, it normally involves some form of planning, whether it is going on a hiking tour or planning a party, wedding, or vacation; we are filled with the excitement, anticipation, and potential fulfillment of the event. The actual participation in these events gets to the core of our pleasure centers. These fulfilling occasions can be called the spice-of-life events, but they come and go with the ebullient flow of time. Obviously we should and, in most cases, do cherish these moments that heighten the bright spots of our lives. However, in a manner of speaking, some of the most rewarding parts of living a peaceful life are the pleasant memories we have from these events. Yes, we should always cherish the moment, but more importantly, we should treasure the memories of these events. The moments in time are temporary, become history, and are seemingly gone in a flash, but memories can be sustainable and last forever, thereby increasing your peace quotient. The compilations of our memories carve out a path that makes life worthwhile and essential to peaceful living even while living in pieces. Here's the thing: peace is yours to own, and nobody can take it away unless you allow them to, but the pieces of life come and go like a thief in the night. We all should and must have an appetite for peace. If we do, we will certainly set the stage to enjoy life's comforts and be able to deal with its everyday stresses in peace.

# An Undermining Peace Assemblage

My life's journey incorporates all the comforts of the conscious thought. They include my perceptions, interpretations, intentions, assumptions, and judgments I make on a daily basis. These assemblages of thought have helped me to maintain contentment, but they have also posed a threat to my peace quotient. All of them have a connection to my emotions and are addressed in this book. My challenge was to recognize how easy it is to be deceived by these thought processes and to regulate the emotional components of my psychological development in order to circumvent the impulses derived from a negative point of view. Not all of my responses are based on emotions or the way I feel at the moment, but my emotions have strongly influenced my actions and directly or indirectly played a crucial role toward living in peace.

Living in peace requires being aware of how you interpret the world around you and, more importantly, how you react to what you perceive to be true or real. If you consistently see things in a negative light, your mental capacity to view things in their proper perspective will be skewed, and in many cases result in unnecessary stress for you and possibly others. If your tendency to interpret what people say or do is always intentional, or viewed with negative lenses, you will find yourself creating an environment of tension and stress unwittingly. For example, if someone steps on your toe and it is painful, how you react to this particular incident will most likely depend on how you interpret the incident. In other words, your perception of whether or not the incident was intentional or unintentional will probably influence your response. Therefore, it is important to distinguish accidental from intentional actions and be mindful of those who often interpret every bump or slight as an intentional act of hostility. If the behavior is deliberate, it is intentional and usually comes from the heart and soul. If your intentions are genuine and flow from love, you have positioned yourself to enjoy a peaceful life. From this vantage, you are confident about your actions because your motives are pure. But if your conduct is suspect and streams from impure motives, you have unconsciously set yourself up for backfire, like a premature explosion in a car engine. However, both intentional and unintentional behaviors have consequences.

Unintentional actions may also be the result of ignorance

or simply accidental but could produce either positive or negative results. Sometimes people are just plain ignorant to the facts. I'm not trying to imply they themselves are ignorant, but what I'm postulating is people are sometimes misguided by false information, or they simply possess limited knowledge on a given subject matter. In these unique instances, they are functioning through ignorance, which can unknowingly sabotage their peace. A known adage "ignorance is bliss" or "what you don't know won't hurt you" may be true under certain circumstances and may allow someone to have peace but only in the short term. The premise is this, if someone is not aware of something, does not have all the facts, or just simply doesn't know what they don't know when carrying out an act, they, at that moment, may likely have peace. But the results, again, can be the same as when their thoughts and actions are knowledge based.

There are many other problems that can be introduced through self-indulgent acts that will affect your peace quotient. If you believe or think you can tell what someone's intentions are before investigating their actions, you are unintentionally undermining the outcome and setting yourself up for an uncontested free-fall of uncertainties and unbounded results. No one can read your mind or determine what your true motives are, but if the tendency is to do so, it is a trap that can consequentially cause unintended discord and damage relationships. It is very difficult to maintain peace under these dimensions of thought. Another way to introduce and undermine your peace is when you prejudge others. If you consistently prejudge without forethought, you are unlikely, in many cases, to be accurate in your assessment, and you will unconsciously introduce an element of uncertainty, which can unnecessarily cause conflicts between you and others. It is fundamentally a truism that our impressions and perceptions are undoubtedly real to us, but they may not be reality based. In other words, our perceptions can lead to inappropriate responses in a host of situations.

You can also undermine your inner peace when you consistently make assumptions about your circumstances and others. Some of us have the benign tendency to overlook and ignore the premise from which we base our assumptions. I would venture to guess most of us do not give this much thought. Many of us seem to conduct our lives treating our thoughts with impunity, as if we are always right, and failing to give consideration that we may be wrong in many instances. Under these circumstances, we are unconsciously and temporarily deprived of logical reflections. Ultimately, intentional misconduct, premature judgments, and thoughtless assumptions, if not put into check, will breed constant disruption in your peace quotient. It is important to remember your actions and decisions, no matter how big or small, can have a profound impact on your life. The crux of the matter is this: by not giving much forethought or seriousness to what you say, what you do, and the conclusions you make, you can create tension in your life and cause distress to others. Thus, you cannot consistently live apeaceful life under this determination.

There are many internal struggles we all must face and overcome. The struggles can come in many ways, such as taking things too personally, holding grudges, or being unforgiving. With these infractions of the mind, we become captive to our own self-induced world of conflict and discord. But just as pernicious, I see four basic human tendencies we engage in that can prominently sabotage any ability to live in peace consistently. They are fear, insecurity, doubt, and pride. Fear denotes attributes of despair, alarm, anxiety, and disquietude, which disables your ability to function in hope. It can paralyze you in many ways and keep you from living out your dreams, but hope gives the assurance of a positive outcome. Insecurity is a form of being detached, having no boundaries or refuge, and grounded by a lack of confidence in yourself. It can and will undermine your ability to be at peace. Doubt is indecision on steroids and is the opposite of belief, which is the cornerstone of certainty, conviction, and faith. The presence of doubt will always compromise your resolve to get things done.

Pride can be viewed positively, such as having pride in your work ethic or being proud of someone else's accomplishments. But pride in its purest form has all the elements of arrogance, conceit, and vanity. It is one aspect of our nature that can prevent us from being humble. Without humility, we are destined to fall. Although all of us have the above tendencies, the challenge is to understand how they can impair our ability to have peace, face them squarely, and overcome them with conviction.

# Introspection of Peace

I have contemplated and thought for many years about how powerful our perceptions are and how much they can impact our peace quotient. Every single day, as we conduct our deliberate affairs, we are writing on our hearts how we think, how we feel, and how we may satisfy or sabotage our primal existence. From the time we are born to the time we reach the end of our lives, we internalize our surroundings to be true or real, but we fail to recognize the collaborative fallacies we store in our hearts to validate or invalidate what we think or feel. The fallacies are simply derived perceptions from our primary senses—what we see, what we hear, what we taste, what we smell, and what we touch. We live through the lens of these senses, but we fail to consciously consider what we see is sometimes different from what others see, or what we hear may be in discord with others, or what we taste depends primarily on an individual's palate, or what we smell to be pleasant to one individual may be repugnant to another, or what we touch can be perceived differently by others. We are all different, but our senses and emotions are the gateway to peaceful living, and through these lens, we are able to live a healthy and stable life. However, through the same lens, we can create unhealthy relations and cause discontentment. I'm not saying there is anything inherently wrong with our emotions or senses; they are God-given. But what I am postulating is that our perceptions, based on the lens from which we view things, can have a considerable impact on our lives. This is the case because what we perceive through our senses to be true, in every instance, may not be reality based. This is important to note because if we, in fact, perceive everything to be real or true to us, our subconscious will accept rather than reject the premise from what we conceive to be truth, even if it's not. We will therefore react to that perceived reality. Based on how close a perception is to reality will sometimes govern whether or not the response is appropriate or inappropriate. An appropriate response will most likely result in contentment, lending to a peaceful outcome, but an inappropriate response will probably cause misunderstanding, reinforcing the inevitable pieces we encounter during our lives. Through the senses, we observe many things, and as we perceive, we will obviously react or respond to a given situation. The way we feel covers a considerable range of emotions, such as guilt, anger, sadness, joy, and grief. The reactions or responses, in many cases, driven by emotions, can help to improve or destroy a moment. Consideration should always be given to the possibility that how we respond or react to the way we feel may hurt one person but not hurt another. A response to either of these emotions can determine an appropriate or inappropriate action. Therefore, our emotions, coupled with the senses alone, can protect us from physical harm but can also psychologically sabotage a potential peaceful life. This proposition before us suggests we do, in fact, have control of whether or not we have peace in our lives.

## The Peace Intruders

There are numerous famous philosophers who have talked about knowing yourself and knowing who the enemy is, usually discussed in the context of conflicts or wars. Before you can access your peace quotient, you must first know who the enemy is and what the enemy represents. Our enemy, in this case, is what I call the peace intruder. Peace intruders are the many bad things that happen in life and your worst advisory for peace. It is literally impossible to avoid living in pieces because there will always be peace intruders. They can rob you of your life's quest for contentment, if you allow them. The peace intruder could be a simple disagreement with someone or a longterm friendship gone sour. It could be a drawn-out illness of a close relative or close friend or even death in your family. A financial crisis is a peace intruder. An inability to control anger can be a peace intruder or allowing someone, through words, to disturb your peace. A failure of some kind or an abandonment of trust can be considered peace intruders. All of the above can and will affect the quality of your life, but you certainly have the ability to determine and therefore regulate your peaceful quotient. Peace intruders can come in many forms but can be quelled by simply acknowledging the obvious stress points and knowing yourself. The stress points are the situations that cause you to worry and the circumstances that make you feel uncomfortable. Knowing who you are can inoculate you from the garbage being thrown at you, on a daily basis, and from the worthless attempts of your own sometimes-uninformed thinking that makes your life comfortless. If you don't know yourself or who the intruder is, it will sabotage your peace most of the time. If you know yourself but do not know who the intruder is, it will rob you of your peace on many occasions. Although the peace intruder is a fact of life, it is transient. Therefore, if you know who you are as well as who the intruder is, your peace will rarely be taken away. Knowing yourself and what the peace intruder represents is critical to your well-being because you will clearly be able to recognize and understand the cyclical nature of this advisory. In this case, your mind will be in the best place to accept the good and bad events in life, without reservation.

# CHAPTER 3
## The Genesis of My Peace

My JOURNEY IN LIFE BEGAN in the early 1950s with birth through my mother and father whom I owe so much. They have been an inspiration to me and have influenced my life more than anyone I know except my wife and God. After recently celebrating their sixty-fifth anniversary, it is amazing to see how devoted they are to each other and how they managed to cultivate a relationship for so many years. I am especially thankful they stayed together as they treaded troubled waters through financial hardships, illnesses, and personal conflicts, which all lasting marriages have to bear. Both my mother and father came from very humble beginnings, raised in the Deep South of Mississippi with very few resources to begin a marriage. I am one of three sons and the fifth of seven children. I have two "stepsisters and one stepbrother" who were born by a different father. My mother married her first husband who passed at an early age. My mother remarried and then came along my brother, me and two younger sisters. Although I referred my older sisters and brother as "stepchildren" I don't see them that way. I consider them now and have always recognized them as flesh and blood sisters and bother as I do my siblings from my father. We grew up together and that was all I knew for a long time before I realized they had a different father. My father also treated them as if they were his own. Neither my mother nor my father graduated high school, but both have prodigious common sense, which I have not seen too often even with so-called educated folks. They moved to St. Louis, Missouri, in the late 1940s to raise seven kids (four girls and three boys). They were not wealthy but gave us the best of what they had to give. They provided us, firsthand, with what a family should look like and gave us the moral compass of how we should conduct our lives. They provided us adequate shelter, clothed us as best they could, and always made sure food was available. My parents taught us, from their actions, that success was not solely financial gains but, more importantly, derived from love and compassion. By example, they taught us family was the nucleus of the society, and everything else stemmed from that embryo.

I was about six years old when we moved into our first house. It was an old house but in my impressionable mind appeared to be new. It also captured a new beginning for our growing family and refreshing change from the previous apartment complex where we had lived. To me, it was a step up from the past. Our new house was located in the middle of the block just across the street from an old abandoned building surrounded by a seemingly huge lot. It was a two-story home with separate front and rear entrances. We lived on the first story while some other relatives lived on the second story of the house. There were only two relatively small bedrooms inside our home but still enough room for the nine of us. My two brothers and I stayed in one of the bedrooms. We were young enough to manage sleeping in bunk beds. Two other younger sisters slept in the other bedroom. My two older sisters slept in an open room across from the bathroom and adjacent to the kitchen. My parents slept in a larger room next to the living room, which was near the front entrance into the house. The tight living quarters was not considered an issue for me because we were living in a home we could call our own. This gave me a sense of stability and security, which contributed to a calm and peaceful start in life.

We lived in a neighborhood where everyone on our block knew one another, including the parents of our friends. They also contributed to the well-being of the neighborhood. By nightfall, my mother would make sure her kids were in the house, which meant being inside when the streetlights came on. This was somewhat unsettling for us because many of our neighborhood friends were able to stay out and play while my siblings and I were summoned to come inside the home. On several occasions, my mother would gather all of us around the table at night and tell us stories about her childhood and other fables about life. She gave us a little freedom to roam around the neighborhood but would also monitor each of us like the proverbial plague that leeches to its subjects without discrimination. In retrospect, her diligence to protect us paid off because many people within our community eventually encountered bouts with the criminal justice system, and some of them did not reach adulthood, due to premature deaths for one reason or another.

## Memorable Times and Traditions

My parents made a tradition of keeping the family together, especially by celebrating holidays. They were peaceful gatherings that set the stage for my peaceful upbringing. These observances were obviously special, highlights of my childhood, and serve as good memories. About three or four times during the summer, my parents would take the family to picnic at local parks for good times. Thanksgiving was a special time to be thankful. My father would, for several years, buy a live turkey and feed and fatten it to be enjoyed during our Thanksgiving meal. Easter was also memorable because, in addition to commemorating Jesus's resurrection, we would get a set of new clothes for church. Believe me, this was huge to us kids. Christmas was probably the most precious time of the year to our family. While acknowledging the birth of Christ, we would all give and be given gifts as we gathered together opening toys and exchanging gifts on Christmas day. These were family times together that cannot be forgotten. These were also times when we would become more bonded with close relatives, which created an environment of trust and goodwill. As we got older, we would spend more time with extended family members while celebrating the various holidays. Even during these times of my life, there were struggles and difficulties, along with physical, psychological, and painful challenges I had to face growing up.

## My Parents' Influence and Diligence

My mother and father had a great impact on my life, and they both contributed to why I have been able to live my life in peace.

My mother worked at a hospital as a technician while being the caretaker, providing most of the discipline and structure to keep the family together. At the time, my grandmother lived with us as well and also provided guidance and discipline. My mother showed me how to love unconditionally through the sacrifices she made for me. She was always available to me when I needed her. Even with her own imperfections, she made sure I could fend for myself once I left home to raise my own family. She taught me how to clean the house, as well as to cook, wash, iron, and sew my clothes. She was a master of these chores and left no stones unturned. When there was a problem, she would be by my side to console and comfort me, letting me know that all would be well. She made many sacrifices for me and my brothers and sisters, which taught me to do the same. When I was hit by a car at four years old, my mother was one of the first on the scene. When I spilled hot grease on my chest at age five, she was there to assure me everything would be all right. When I fell on an iron rod that pierced my knee at seven years old, my mother was there to console me.

My father worked the nightshift for many years, providing most of the household's financial support. He played a different role in my life, in that he had a quiet and peaceful countenance about him. He was down to earth, always exhibited a balanced approach to life, and was always calm during seemingly rough times. He also demonstrated to me a work ethic by his working long hours to provide for our family. He was rarely overbearing and taught me how to be a patient father by allowing me to make some mistakes on my own. My parents were my role models. They embodied a spirit of compassion, simplicity, and structure. These notable characteristics were what, I feel, my parents placed before me even with their many imperfections. My parents' existence lives through me, and my story is embedded in them, but the true author of my story is God. My mother and father are now deceased but lived to see five generations from their union. My mother was ninety one years old when she passed and my father passed at ninety eight years of age. May they rest in peace.

# CHAPTER 4
## Emergence of My Peace and Pieces

Born IN 1951, I WAS raised in St. Louis, Missouri, and lived in a relatively poor neighborhood with lower-middle class characteristics. I am a middle child and grew up with six other siblings — Jimmie and Alice (two older sisters), Robert and Sammie Jr. (two older brothers), and Shirley and Stephanie (two younger sisters). I was a very frightened little boy, not by people, but I was afraid of ghosts and dead people. My mother attended a lot of funerals when I was growing up. I hated funerals and thought the deceased could or may rise from the dead which sent shivers through my spine. On several occasions, my mother would sit us around the kitchen table after dinner and tell us ghost stories. The thought of dead people and ghost were very terrifying to me as a child and were magnified by personal experiences. I was about 4 years old when I saw a dead man lying on the sidewalk in front of our next-door neighbor's house. At seven years old, I witnessed the crib death of my oldest sister's first child of three months old in the home where we lived. From these experiences, I would have nightmares which seemed to bring the fear of the dead and ghosts alive.

I was also afraid to cheat, lie, steal, or use vulgar language because I was taught not to and thought if I did I would go to hell and languish in fire with brimstones forever when I died. My reverence to God and other childhood experiences influenced my thinking and I believe set the stage for me to want peace in my life. As I got older, some of these small but impactful thoughts about fear gradually disappeared.

## The Fallen Nature

I am a prime example of our fallen nature, and it began as early as the toddler's stage. For example, I was severely injured three times before I reached the age of eight, primarily because I didn't do what I had been taught. When I was only four years old, I was hit by a car, even after constantly being told to look out for cars before running into the streets. This incident occurred when I followed an older sister, brother, and cousin dashing across the street going to an uncle's house. They made it across the street, but I did not. I recall lying on the street's pavement with people watching as I regained consciousness from being hit by the car. For the first time, I could hear the distant sound of a siren from an ambulance approaching to whisk me off to the hospital. I sustained a concussion and spent many nights at the local hospital. I'm sixty-four years old, and sixty years later, I clearly remember this incident and will never forget it. Unfortunately, this particular accident did not deter me from being disobedient and making other bad judgments.

One year later, I sustained third-degree burns when I spilled hot grease onto, mainly, my chest. I had clearly been told to stay away from fire and not to play around or touch anything hot, near or on the stove. For some reason, this did not register in my mind. One evening my mother had just finished cooking a meal. She poured very hot grease into a can and placed it on the stove. As soon as she turned her back, through curiosity, I reached up and grabbed the container of hot grease. The grease spilled onto parts of my face and chest. I was five years old. I don't remember this incident, but I know it happened because I have a permanent scar on my chest, over my heart, which will remain until I die. Again, through my own disobedience and stubborn nature, I was severely injured and sustained third-degree burns. I remember lying in the hospital bed feeling lonely and abandoned, especially at night. I remember hearing the trains go by in the wee hours of night, wondering when I would return home. As I look back, these two incidents were very troubling because they remind me of how disobedient I was at such an early age. When I was about seven and a half years old, my mother told me and two brothers not to play near an abandoned building called the huts, but we did anyway. As with many youngsters at those ages, we didn't believe our mother would ever know we had disobeyed her or would ever find out. The huts was right across the street from our house with an open lot about a block long. The lot was covered with weeds, broken glass, rocks, cans, and iron rods coming out of the ground. While running and playing hide and go seek on the lot, I fell on an iron rod that went about an inch or two into the soft part of my knee. My brothers saw me fall and rushed me to the house. The flush feeling that came over me and the amount of blood gushing from my knee was overbearing. As the blood ran profusely from my leg, I remember being very frightened, saying to my mother, "I don't want to die." She of course assured me I would be okay. I received about twelve stitches from this incident and can't blame anyone but myself. The fact I was severely injured three times before the tender age of eight is a testament to my aberrant nature, but God had his hands on my life. However, these were just the beginnings of a long history of injuries. By the time I reached my teens, I had sustained head injuries, broken and fractured bones, and many injuries requiring stitches. These events were part and parcel of my childhood experiential pieces.

## Invisible Wounds

Sometimes our problems are obvious, and other times they are not. My childhood was troubled with low self-esteem and inferior thoughts about myself. I felt like the black sheep of the family and left out on many things. I also felt unloved, especially compared to my brother, Sammie Jr., who is one year older than I. I felt he was preferred over me because of his looks—lighter skin complexion and curlier hair. Although I have no concrete proof, I believe my youngest sister, Stephanie, probably felt the same way as I did, growing up with a sister one year older who seemed to have been favored over her. While living in a household with two older brothers, I would unconsciously compare myself to them and, in many cases, felt they were always better than I. To me, they were smarter, had more athletic prowess, and had better judgment. Even though I have always been impressed with my oldest brother, Robert, I rarely compared myself to him. He seemed to be many years older than I and was, to me, way out of my league. However, my brother Sam seemed to have been stronger, better looking, and wiser than I. I don't remember anyone telling this to me, but that's how I felt emotionally. In my mind, he could do no wrong, and there seemed to surface a self-fulfilling prophecy that he was simply a better person than I.

My initial thought processes began very early in life, probably about age six or seven. From the time my brother and I started school, up to about my second grade, Sam would come home with a nearly perfect report card, and I would bring home very poor grades. This lasted a couple years until my father got into the act. One occasion when I came home with a bad report card, my father took me to the side and admonished me not to bring home another bad report card. I don't recall his exact words, but I took his words seriously enough that, from that day forward, I never brought home another report card reflecting the poor academic performance I had in the past. The real issue wasn't my brother being much smarter but that he obviously took school seriously and I did not. However, my belief that he was smarter than I was had already been etched into my little unsophisticated mind. I have the utmost respect and love for my brother, and he has never said or done anything harmful to me. But in my mind, I felt that he and everyone else, including my parents, thought more of him than they thought of me. This state of mind was a personal internal struggle for me, including my perception of what others thought about me compared to him. As a result, I would do things unconsciously, causing psychological pain and, in some cases, physical injuries.

My hospital sojourns during my adolescence bear testament to how damaging perceptions can be. The inferior thoughts and low self-esteem issues were manifested through destructive behavior; however, these issues were the tip of the iceberg. Deeper within my consciousness was also a hidden complex that followed me into adulthood, which I believe began when I was in the second or third grade. The teacher took a picture showing the side of the students' heads. Each student cut out his own picture and placed black paper over it, which created a silhouette image of our heads. The image of each student's head shape was posted on a wall. I don't remember the reason for this exercise, but as I saw the other classmates' profiles, there were all shapes and sizes, but none were like mine. This was the first time I actually saw the shape of my head from a side view. I was embarrassed by the shape of my head because the back of my head looked flat. It looked as if someone had chopped the back of my head in half with an ax. This particular classroom assignment was disheartening and the first time in my life when I began to be self-conscious of my appearance. It manifested a profound sense of unquestionable awareness and was unfortunately reinforced by insensitive comments from kids my age, friends and foes alike, who called me flat head. This also added to the initial psychological scars I had already developed from thinking I was inferior to others.

This thing was huge in my mind, and I needed a rational reason for why my head was flat. To find the answer, I asked my mother for an explanation, and she gave one that seemed to be reasonable but didn't help my imposing thoughts. She told me my head was shaped that way because I always slept on my back as a tiny infant. She also tried to comfort me by stating I was well behaved and rarely cried, unlike my other siblings. At such a young age, it was hard for me to accept, but through God's grace and my ignorance, I maintained peace and eventually learned coping skills to disentangle the impact on my emotional stability. However, the name-calling continued throughout my adolescent years, which made me feel very uncomfortable and insecure, but I would always conceal how I actually felt. As I saw it, the best way to conceal the shape of my head was to wear a hat, and I did at all times, in or outside the house, even though I had been taught it was inappropriate to wear a hat when I entered my home or building. Wearing a hat was one of the ways, I believed, I could escape and cope with this huge psychological impediment. I lived with the shame of this hidden wound for many years but did not understand until later in life that my shame was from pride, subterfuge by my own vanity. As I matured and conceptually understood how trivial it was to dwell on my physical appearance, I adjusted to the fact that my head was a small physical imperfection and had nothing to do with who I really am. However, these invisible wounds impacted my thinking before I finally reconciled that I was not unique in that regard. Overtime, I understood that everyone has to cope with each of his own imperfections and that they are by-products of living in pieces.

By the time I reached twelve years of age, the manifestations of my negative thinking had become a stronghold in my life because I actually began to act the part, as if my brother was smarter, stronger, and more attractive. I internalized these to be truth, and I unconsciously began to draw attention to myself by doing foolish things. I didn't understand why at the time, but these acts of silliness were the result of my own internal combustion. My thoughts led me to believe I was unattractive, unintelligent, and clumsy. These issues, I believe, were derived from what I internalized through a unique emotional and psychological lens, but they were just as real to me as the day and night.

## Different Perspectives/Perceptions

In my early teens, I also began to realize that people would see the same things but interpret them differently. For instance, friends and I would frequently go to the movies, return home, and talk about what we saw. It was interesting to hear each of us talk about various parts of the movie we had just watched together, but on many occasions, one or more would recount parts of what they saw differently from what I saw. The different interpretations would always fascinate me. At that point, I began to realize, and assimilate in my mind, the dynamics of other people's perspectives. I imagined the different views of others to be solely guided and driven by their own perceptions. I began to process and concede, in a primitive way, that a personal internalization of the environment played a significant role in differentiating how people think and feel, even while looking through the same lens. I also gained the awareness that a person's perception, reality based or not, will generally govern their behavior and judgments. After being mindful of this idea, I could partly understand and appreciate the complexities of human behavior, which, in part, enabled me to have peace of mind when dealing with people's attitudes and sometimes seemingly peculiar behavior. Even then, I began to understand and recognize we all have character flaws, personality dispositions, and idiosyncrasies. This somewhat primitive understanding of human nature was strangely comforting because of my own internal thought processes, which sometimes appeared to be unconventional.

I was taught many things growing up, as most of us are — including simple things like obeying my parents and others who had charge over my well-being. Being honest and being thoughtful of others were high on my conduct list. I was pretty much convinced of and captivated by the idea that I should treat people like I wanted to be treated, which made a lot of sense to me. In addition, avoiding the immoral acts of lying, cheating, and stealing were basic to my conscious thoughts. These, in my mind, were core principles to live by, and I did my best to do the right things. However, it is obvious, through man's fallen human nature, I, as many of us, do not necessarily or completely live by what we are taught.

## Start but Rarely Finish

Even in the midst of my troubled behavior patterns, there were compensating aspects of my life, which included my athletic ability and potential. Within the community at large, there were many sporting activities for young people like myself. From the time I was eight years old and years beyond, prior to high school, I participated in a number of different intermural sporting activities. I played softball, football, and basketball in an organized league. Before entering high school in 1965, I was also involved with track and field in the local community and other special events. While in elementary school, I learned how to tumble, and I was involved with an inner city form of gymnastics. I learned how to march, and I became a drill team member. I even tried fencing for a while. As a member of a drill team, I participated in several drilling events throughout the city of St. Louis, which was very popular during that time. By the time I reached high school, others and I were selected to teach drilling techniques at various community centers within and outside the St. Louis city limits. During high school, although I was athletically inclined, well built, and had developed the agile ability to engage in any sports endeavor, I was relatively short. Because of this fact, I was somewhat intimidated to join certain high school team sports, such as football, baseball, and especially basketball. My four years of high school were seasoned with many ambivalent experiences. I made good and bad choices. I was not popular in high school but was well known in the circles of high school musicians. I was always good at many sports, which boosted my self-esteem, but I never continued in any one particular sport to exploit my true abilities. For example, I tried out and successfully made the high school's swimming, wrestling, and track teams but never gave chance for a promising future in those sporting activities before quitting. These were a few highlights of my high school accomplishments, but I would get bored quickly before trying another challenge. For example, I was encouraged to join the track team through the insistence of a physical education teacher who believed I had potential. I ran the 440-yard dash or quarter mile for a little over a year before giving up on it. My coach pushed me pretty hard, but I didn't mind because I enjoyed the sport. During many meets, I would be first until a little over halfway around the track when runners passed me, and I would come in third or fourth place in the race. I was always exhausted after every meet because I ran like a rabbit, never properly pacing myself. I rationalized that I simply did not have the endurance that other runners had.

During my second year, before summer break, my coach suggested I run cross-country. I promised I would train but didn't because I really was not interested in running cross-country and I didn't want to interrupt my summer break. Therefore, during the break, I never showed up for cross-country training, and when I returned to school, I was too embarrassment to continue running. I was not proud of the choice I made because of my pride, and he never sought me out. I never spoke to the coach again, and therefore, track and field ended for me. Quitting these activities before enjoying the true essence of my potential as an athlete was obviously a pattern of mine. However, I have always enjoyed an unyielding level of contentment.

# CHAPTER 5
## • • • • • • • • • • • • •
## Boundaries of Peace and Pieces

THE CONSOLIDATION OF MY PEACE while enduring the pieces in my life has been a constant reminder of my joy and my blessings. I got my first job at the age of thirteen, working during the summer at an elementary school doing odd jobs. In my middle teens, I sold fruit and vegetables door to door, and in my late teens, I worked at a small lumber shop in the neighborhood, bundling wood strips after school hours. During my senior year of high school, I worked at the St. Louis Record Center, one of the largest buildings in the country for housing public records and documents. While still in high school, my older brother and sisters with small children would frequently ask me to babysit their young kids, which I, quite frankly, enjoyed doing.

My behavior was remarkably unhinged in 1969, shortly before graduating high school. I started drinking alcohol, which I believe stemmed from a negative perception of myself. My self-inflicted thoughts were not only caused by low self-esteem but also the conscious awareness of nearby areas of poverty, crime, and segregation. The neighborhood where I grew up was just blocks from a large urban housing complex called the Pruitt-Igoe Project. This urban area, about thirty-three eleven-story apartment buildings located on the lower north side of town, was probably one of the most infamous public housing projects ever built in the United States in the early fifties. Prior to its decline in the midsixties, there was unrest and violence, which made for an un-peaceful experience, considering its close proximity to where I lived. I went to high school with many of these folks, who were just as uncomfortable with the situation in which they found themselves as those living in my neighborhood and other surrounding areas. Although my consciousness was raised through this predicament of circumstances, the constant hearing of crime and murders was very unsettling. Even as the upheaval and turmoil in my community persisted, it was reflective of and reinforced by society at large. Growing up and being a teenager before the dawn of the civil rights movement was, by anyone's standard, somewhat tumultuous. I clearly recall the racial strife that engulfed this country's ambivalences and the racial animosity toward African Americans. The deliberate oppression we consistently faced during the sixties, prior to my reaching full manhood, was also embedded into my consciousness. Although proud to be an American citizen, while enjoying the freedoms and liberties we now have, it was painful enough to personally experience racism and especially disconcerting hearing the stories about the real history of this country's allowance of the hideous miscarriage of justice and discriminatory practices. I was too young, in some cases, to witness or experience some of them but could clearly comprehend things were afoul during many periods of unrest. For decades, much of the country was segregated. Blacks were kept separate from whites, banned from attending most white schools, barred from sitting in the front of buses, forbidden to swim in public pools, assigned separate water fountains from which to drink and different restrooms. This was all jarring to my developing conscious state of mind. Even before learning the true history of my people's ancestry and this country's part in undermining our rights, we were engaged in an educational system that deprived us of our numerous contributions to this country's history. Because of this fact, we now have black history month, which is regretful but sorely needed because our true history has been parsed for so long. When I became of age to understand and realize what was going on with continual rampant discrimination, I could sense the emotional drain by many blacks and the resulting psychological impact on many of us who felt inferior to whites.

It was a challenge for many of us to overcome these shackles and maintain sanity. Although St. Louis stayed calm while other cities were rioting during the sixties, I do recall one unsettling incident that occurred in my neighborhood. It began between a certain family and the police but quickly escalated when young people in the area joined, and the police called in reinforcements, which resulted in many injured policeman and their dogs. Many police cars were damaged as well. I was not at the scene, but my older sister Alice witnessed it all. Apparently, as the incident became unmanageable, tear gas was thrown, reaching the street where we lived. This was the first and only time I can recall ever experiencing the imposing effects of tear gas. I was also in my teens when John F. Kennedy, Malcolm X, and later Dr. Martin Luther King Jr. and Robert Kennedy were killed, all of whom died during the sixties. During this period, my internal struggles of ambivalence and how I fit into the larger society took a while to reconcile. These were disturbing times. Even long after Jim Crow laws were abolished and the Civil Rights Act of 1957 had become law, blacks were still facing discrimination in housing and employment. During this period of my life, civil unrest, in this country, seemed more prevalent. Frankly speaking, police brutality and abuse was not very much different then from what it is today.

## Unfortunate Police Encounter

I recall, in the early seventies, while still in the navy, I returned home on leave and experienced one of the most terrifying events of my life. One of my best friends, a musician who was invited to play with a band at Scott Air Force base in Illinois, asked me to join him. We grew up together and played in the same high school band and R&B group. As we traveled about fifty miles on a rainy cool night, to find the spot where we would be jamming, we got lost and couldn't find the exact location where the event was to be held. After driving around a bit and being unfamiliar with this particular environment, we decided to ask someone for more precise directions but were unknowingly given the run around. The area was predominately white, where very few blacks lived. It seemed to have been minutes after following the directions we were given before we reached a particular intersection and found ourselves surrounded by police cars. The police car lights were glaring from all sides. Guns were pointed directly at the vehicle we were in. The moment we stopped, from a bullhorn we were told, "Get out of the car." I was driving and had no chance to put my gear in park because my hands were raised. Quite frankly, I was afraid if I did, they would fire their weapons. Their guns were pointed at us while they demanded us to exit the vehicle. To say the least, we were frightened beyond disbelief because we both thought if we made the slightest move, we would be fired upon. I hesitated for a brief second and put the gear into park. The officer shouted again and again, "Exit the vehicle." We both had a decision to make, either take the chance of being fired upon while inside the car or be fired upon once we got out of the car. I thought our lives would be ended that night. The uncertainty was deafening as my life flashed by momentarily. I finally summoned the courage to get out of the car, and my friend did as well. As soon as we exited the car, the police officers surrounded us and demanded us to step away from the car. We did what we were told without even knowing why we were stopped in the first place. When one of us summoned the courage to ask the simple question, what did we do and why were we stopped, the officers ignored our curiosity, viewing us as though we were being disrespectful or uncooperative. At this point, an officer said, "Bend over and face the hood of the car", while shortly afterwards handcuffing both of us. An officer was loud and boisterous insisting we lay on the wet ground, facedown, with our hands behind our backs. Again, we complied to their demands and gave them no reason to do us harm. As we lay on the ground, one of the officers shouted, "Don't look up and keep your faces down." When one of us did, another officer slapped our caps off our heads and repeated, "Do as you are told." We were certainly afraid, because we thought for sure our lives were over.

After being on the ground for about twenty minutes or so, we were taken to the police station, and after another twenty minutes, one of them informed us that they had made a mistake. They said the guy who gave us directions intentionally did so and called the police, stating we robbed a gas station, and he gave a description of the car and clothes we were wearing. After the police questioned this individual, he confessed to stealing money and whatever else had been stolen. We never received an apology, and we never made it to the event.

My intentions are not to demean all police officers, because I have also had positive encounters with them and believe they serve a vital role toward protecting our communities. Suffice to say, my friend and I walked away alive and relieved no harm came to us. He and I have been friends nearly fifty years, and we remain the best of friends today. We grew up together in the same neighborhood, went to the same schools, and hung out together. All my family knows him and treats him like a brother. We have done many things together. He had my back, and I had his. Although we live miles apart and at times may not speak to one another for years, our friendship has held tight. My friend's name is Michael Winston.

Having dependable friendships in your life is relevant to a peaceful life. Many of us will meet and enjoy many acquaintances over the years and will certainly develop friendships, but true friends are hard to find. Having many acquaintances is important, but a true friend is like a golden nugget and should never be taken for granted. At my age, I can count on one hand who my true friends are. A true friend will not hold grudges against you and will always have your best interest at heart. For the most part, I have learned most of the people you meet along your path in life are simply a blend of humanity put here on earth to help you achieve your destiny. I have also concluded that no matter how affirming or toxic my relationships are with others, they serve as an apparatus for my personal growth and for my character building. This concept alone gives me peace of mind.

# CHAPTER 6
## Subsidiary of Peace

My experience in music has been fulfilling and has contributed to my life's peace and contentment. I was in elementary school when I first had any interest in learning to play music. To my knowledge, at the time, I knew of no one in my family's history who played an instrument or for that matter had any musical talent. Years later, I discovered there were several prominent professional musical entertainers in the family.

My interest in music began when I came across an old vintage silver-plated saxophone someone left behind. The saxophone was not in playing condition. It had missing pads, dented keys, chipped mouthpiece, and a couple cracked reeds. I didn't have a dime to fix it, but I tried to play it anyway. This old vintage instrument was the impetus to my becoming interested in playing a musical instrument, so I joined my elementary school band while in the seventh grade. I knew absolutely nothing about notes, scales, or fingering for the saxophone or any other instrument but experimented playing the tuba, violin, and saxophone, none of which I stuck with because I quit for some unknown reason.

Prior to beginning high school, I made a choice to join the high school choir instead of the high school band in my freshman year because the band would require certain expenses I thought I could not afford. This was not a major decision but one that was not well thought out because I joined the band in the beginning of my sophomore year in high school anyway. The high school band program's instrumental musical sequence was comprised of three different levels—one year of beginning band, another year in the intermediate or junior band, and the following year in the senior band. Although I had very little knowledge of music, I quickly learned the fundamentals, skipped the junior band, and was moved to the senior band after one year in the beginning band. By that time, my love and passion for music had swelled to a point I knew playing music would be a big part of my life. My high school academic performance was average, and I rarely excelled to those higher levels of achievements because I just didn't take school as seriously as I should have. I didn't care for American history that much, had little interest in reading, and was average in math. My primary interests, by far, were the indulgence in sports and playing a musical instrument.

I grew up having a passion for music and continue to this day, but my expression of music through playing the sax has been tenuous at best. My last year of high school was probably my best because I had become a little more known as a fairly good athlete and had a promising future in music. Things started to look up in music because, while a junior in high school, a friend and fellow senior band member approached me about playing in a rhythm and blues (R&B) band outside of school, and I accepted. Although I had played with my high school's concert, marching, and jazz bands, I had never played music solely by ear. Playing by ear was exciting but a totally new experience. Most bands today are very different than they were when I was growing up. Back in my day, bands were relatively large and plentiful throughout the city of St. Louis. The band I played with, called the Cro'shades, had twelve members, drummer, lead, rhythm, and bass guitars, four-piece horn section, trombone, trumpet, alto and tenor saxes, and four singers. It was a family-run enterprise with most of its members (siblings) being a part of the family. The mother and father were managers and ran the show. We played in small clubs on most weekends throughout the city of St. Louis, which seemed to be the highlight of my music experience at the time.

After playing music a while in the high school band and with the R&B group, I developed such a passion for music that playing music became the center of my life. I wanted to do nothing else but play music. Playing with the high school band was certainly one of the most fulfilling times of my life. My high school's marching band at Vashon was known as one of the best marching bands in the city of St. Louis and even the state of Missouri because we were fortunate enough to have one of the best, if not the best, band director in the city, Mr. Spearmen. Our marching band had become so popular that we were afforded the opportunity to perform during halftime for the St. Louis Cardinals and Atlanta Falcons at the Bush Stadium. This was in the late sixties, and I believe our performance was the first in all the city or state for a high school marching band to perform a halftime show during a professional football team's game. The band had received such recognition throughout the city that by the time my senior class was to graduate, almost every graduating senior band member was offered music scholarships to various colleges. I, for one, received scholarship offers from three different colleges before graduating high school but declined them all to pursue my music career with the R&B band. My decision not to accept the music offers was based on the fact that I didn't want to leave the R&B band and believed we would eventually become successful in the music industry. This decision was the beginning of many major decisions I made that, I believe, set a pattern for my making choices based primarily on current circumstances. The R&B band broke up one year after my high school graduation. I had not anticipated this break up, and, at that point, my pursuit in music with this band was completely shattered. Many band members and I were devastated because we had hoped to make it big in the music industry. At this point, it was unclear what I would do because I had put my future on the line to be part of a successful music group. My desire to continue playing music was nearly crushed because I thought my dream of playing music as a profession would not be realized. Not knowing how difficult it would be for our band to make it big and not considering how volatile the music industry was, I was lured into not accepting the scholarships offers. I was so blinded by a reckless ambition and passion for music that I did not conceive what the future would hold if the band failed to prosper or even penetrate the music industry. In addition, I did not think about or foresee how this one decision I made would impact my future and those to follow. Decision after decision was made because of circumstances I created, which means I had not set a deliberate course for my life's future. I made another major decision to attend Lane College. This was another decision based on my circumstances, not with deliberate thought about my future goals. Lane accepted me as a new incoming student, and I was grateful and thought I had made a good decision by pursuing a college education. I had planned to major in music, but it wasn't long before I received a draft notice from the military. I sought to get a deferment to stay in school, but I was unsuccessful. I was once again faced with another circumstance where I had to make decision. I had a choice to make — either be drafted or quit college and join another branch of military service. In my mind, neither was a choice I liked, but I settled with joining the United States Navy in hopes of becoming a member of the navy's elite band. I had to quickly become mentally prepared for a new adventure after quitting college. The navy, I thought, would be a good fit for me, especially after hearing good things about its band. I therefore rationalized I would essentially begin a new start in life to pursue music, which remained a passion and desire for a long time. I had no idea what my military experience would be like but I was ready and willing to give it my best.

When I enlisted, I was given the opportunity to audition for the band, either before or during boot camp training. I chose the latter for convenience sake. There was no question in my mind I was good enough to make the navy band because of my high school and outside music experience. By the time I was nineteen, I had made three major decisions in my life. It never crossed my mind nor did I give consideration to the fact that the choices I made could have such a profound impact on my future. If I had not rejected the scholarship offers, my life would have taken a totally different future trajectory. It was later in life when I realized how important it was to set concrete goals and plans for my career. I could not see what the future held, and because of this fact, I should have been very careful and should have taken considerable thought about the decisions I made.

As I envisioned playing with the navy band, I was placed in a special unit consisting of band and choir members. Our day began with morning class sessions together and split in the afternoon where band members practiced with the navy band and choir members sang with the navy choir, which is why our companies were considered special units. For approximately thirteen weeks, our activities remained the same. Occasionally our company's band members would play at different events with the navy band in places like Milwaukee and Chicago. We also played at all the graduation ceremonies, which occurred once week. At the end of about twelve weeks of training, my company prepared for its own graduation. At that juncture, I and four other musicians who wanted to be part of the regular navy band were scheduled to audition. Another musician and I played the sax. The three other musicians played the trumpet, trombone, and drums. Each of us auditioned separately. I was the last to audition. As I watched and waited for each musician to be heard, I was comforted that each passed the audition. I had played with them for the past twelve weeks. It was then my turn to audition. Sight-reading was critical to making the navy band, and I was confident because I had played most of the music we practiced and had performed them on many occasions not only with the navy but also in high school. When I began my audition, I was surprised that the music placed before me was not what we had played or practiced over the previous months. I became a little nervous but did my best to pass the audition. When I completed my audition, I was astonished to hear that I did not make the cut. When I heard those words, a thousand thoughts raced quickly through my mind and one in particular—that I was a poor musician. It was devastating to hear that, essentially, I was not good enough for the navy band. I felt my future, as a musician, had just been put to rest, and my not making the band was a complete failure. My ego and pride were shattered to pieces, my dream of being a musician was crushed, and I thought my desire to play music would never be as I had envisioned.

From this experience, I was reminded again of the prior incident when my company's leader position was taken away for no good reason. I actually contemplated whether or not there was a racial component to me not being selected. This idea was more relevant because the other four members who auditioned and who were granted to play with the navy band were white. However, I reserved judgment on this matter because it could not be proven. My primary rationale at the time was that I did not audition well. Of my entire military service, this particular moment was probably the most devastating jolt to my musical abilities. As with many other setbacks, I moved on. My interest and passion in music has never ceased, and to this day, I continue playing my sax with peace of mind.

# CHAPTER 7
## Managing the Peace and Pieces

I WAS IN COLLEGE WHEN I received my draft notice and in a place in my life where I had been told I had a son, whom I unfortunately disowned. I was also perplexed at the idea I needed to make a decision to quit school or accept the draft. This was mentally disconcerting because I couldn't get a deferment to remain in school. I had two choices—either be drafted or join another branch of service for a longer period. I truly did not want to face the perils of a war I knew little about. I'm speaking of the Vietnam War where many brave men and women fought to preserve and protect our country. By the middle sixties, there were many protests and news clips about this particular war and our country's participation in it. I knew very little about how the war started or why we were there. But what I did know, firsthand, were friends and family members who never made it back alive and some who were not mentally stable when they returned. I was still in my teens when my consciousness was raised about the war.

One of my cousins, whom I grew up with, had a promising future ahead of him before he was drafted when he was eighteen years old. He was only a year or two older than I and was drafted shortly after he graduated high school. I knew him well because his family and mine lived together in a two-family complex for a few years. He left for the war and returned two years later, but he was not the same person I knew before he left. He would walk around by himself, for miles, seemingly in a daze. He couldn't hold a job, was mentally unstable, and never received the help he needed. He was not killed in the war, but it essentially killed his promising future. His dream was never fulfilled because of the war. His predicament affected me more than I realized. There were countless other young men from my community who fought in the Vietnam War. Many never returned home, and many who returned were mentally scarred for life. The most perplexing dichotomy about the Vietnam War was that many who bravely served our country and returned home were not welcomed nor given the same treatment as those who fought in previous wars. I did not experience the devastations of war firsthand, but I can appreciate that we are a blessed country because of the brave veterans who fought and gave up their lives for this country. They should always be honored and remembered. My late cousin's name is Arthur Gibson, a true veteran and patriot. RIP.

# First Educational Pursuit

When I was admitted into Lane College in Jackson, Tennessee, in the fall of 1970, I was only able to enter a work-study program to offset part of my tuition. The work-study program involved playing with the college band. As I looked forward to the prospect of majoring in music to continue my passion for music, I was later faced with an unexpected predicament. The troubling part about this predicament was that my parents had to pay most of my tuition, money they really didn't have and could not afford without making an extreme sacrifice. I thought about the earlier decision I made by not following up on scholarship offers; by not doing so, I put a huge burden on my parents. They did the best they could to help.

This was my first time ever leaving home for an extended period. I was afraid and still naive about many things in life. I was afraid because I was about to tread new waters and had doubts about whether or not I would financially be able to complete college, but I knew, with my parents support, I would manage. I recall the first time I entered my dormitory and heard, ringing in the halls, a popular song at the top of the R&B charts in the early seventies, called "Still Waters Run Deep," music by one of the great groups at that time, the Four Tops. That song played in my head for a very long time and to this day always brings back the memories of my very first experience in college.

As I settled in and became familiar with the school's campus layout, I became more relaxed, but I missed being home. The first few weeks of my college experience were made a little easier because three other high school band members who received scholarships when I did were sophomores. It helped me adjust to the environmental change much faster. They were able to coach and guide me as I learned from their freshman experiences. I was naïve when I left home because I had been essentially sheltered from the world and its sometimes- unpredictable perils up to that point.

## Basic Training with Disappointments

I left my hometown for the second time in my life in 1971. I was excited and very hopeful about my future, notwithstanding prior decisions I had made concerning music. I began boot camp training in the cold of March near the Great Lakes of Illinois not far from the Windy City of Chicago. It was during the winter and very cold at camp but intriguing because I looked forward to this new experience. As I settled in for the first few days and became familiar with the camp's routine, I met many young men from all walks of life who, like myself, were ready to forge a new adventure in life without trepidation.

There were two different camps—the first where companies were formed, and the other where the actual training occurred. A day or two after my orientation, I was called to audition for the boot camp band. I passed and was immediately sent to the second camp where my company would gradually be formed. I was the first to arrive and waited for the company to grow to about sixty recruits. This company was one of four special units, consisting of a combination of band and choir members. It took about a week or two to form our company, and being the first member, the company commander appointed me to be the leader of our unit because of my marching and drilling background. Besides the training I had conducted in local community centers while still in high school, this was the first opportunity given to me to actually lead a group of my peers, and I felt gratified for this privilege.

As my company reached its maximum unit capacity, a Caucasian, at least six foot four and one of the last recruits to complete our unit, came aboard and was unceremoniously appointed the leader of the unit. I was, by then, well respected by other company members, white and black, and had done nothing wrong. But my company commander approached and convinced me that the new guy should lead the company. I can't recall what his exact words were, but his reasoning seemed plausible at the time. He then appointed me second in charge of the company, and I accepted this position gracefully. However, the thought of being second in command, especially after leading the company faithfully without a glitch, was a little disheartening. Although I accepted the change in title, deep within my soul I felt insulted and betrayed by my company commander's decision. I was not angry or resentful, but it was difficult to remove from my mind why he felt compelled to change something that was not broken.

I began to have self-doubts and questioned whether or not I had the real capabilities to lead even while I was leading. In the same thought process, I wondered if race had anything to do with the change, but I had no real evidence to support or debunk that notion. Only five of the sixty recruits in my company were African American, including myself. However, over time, it was obvious I was more familiar with the company's routine, and I basically continued to lead the company notwithstanding the title change. Throughout most of our training, the leader position seemed to be in name only because he would lean on me for guidance, and I was essentially the company's mentor and counselor.

We all got along well until the last few weeks before our graduation. It appeared that low-level tension between the company's whites and blacks began to surface in unexpected ways. Black company members would approach me about subtle racial disputes that had never come up in the early part of the thirteen weeks of our living together. Be that as it may, the time in boot camp was a lonely time in my life. Being away from home, family, and friends was truly an isolated experience. The only comforting part of my loneness while in basic training was when I occasionally received mail from my mom. I have never told her this, but she helped me survive the loneliness and isolation I felt for nearly six months.

## Holding Company of Missteps

After graduating basic training, I was one of three who did not get orders for the next duty station and was placed in what was called a holding company. This was very unsettling to me because my mind had been set on getting my deserved two weeks' leave to spend with my family, whom I had not seen in three months. I was not given any options, and there was no guarantee of how long it would take to get orders for my next duty station. I was very disappointed and, without giving much thought, living in pieces because of the uncertainty.

About thirty others including myself were being held in holding company. Since we were boot camp graduates, we were granted certain privileges we didn't have during boot camp training. The training was regimented where we received no liberties off base. However, in the holding company, we had special liberties to go off base during the week and the weekends.

We worked together and carried out certain duties requiring us to clean and maintain the barracks' appearance and other light chores given when needed. Although we remained at the same location where we trained, we had our meals at a different eating facility called a mess hall. These privileges made life a little more tolerable for most of us, and we rarely complained, until, for some unknown reason, our liberties began to be gradually taken away. They began to restrict our liberty hours to almost nonexistent and curtailed other freedoms we were originally allowed to have. By this time, most of us had already been held for more than a month but still had no idea when our orders would come. As we complained about our rights, they appeared to fall on deaf ears. The last straw occurred about two months after having been held in the holding company. Early one morning, about six or seven of us went to eat breakfast, as we did many times in the past. However, this particular time, we were told we could no longer eat at that particular mess hall. We were told that from then forward we had to eat with the regular recruits. We were not given any explanation, and we felt this abrupt change was unfair. By this time, all of us had already felt mistreated, and frustration had begun to set in. This decision was difficult to accept, and we resisted by declaring we were not leaving until we had our meal. The folks at the mess hall were, I'm sure, only doing as they were told, but it didn't matter to us. We became belligerent that morning, and we turned over tables, chairs, and anything that got in our way. Unfortunately, this was not the right thing to do or the way to respond. I can in no way justify my response or the actions of others who participated in this riotous act. Thankfully, no one got hurt, but there was a lot of damage to the mess hall. Never in my life had I ever displayed such destructive behavior. It seemed as if everything came to a tipping point through my own frustration. I felt that I had no control of my life and that all of my rights had been stripped from me. Imagine someone having total control of your entire existence while dictating when and where you can go, what you do, and how to do it. That's how I felt, and the frustration I personally felt quickly reached a critical point where I really didn't care what happened to me at that particular moment.

This incident reminded me of the riots that took place in many major cities throughout this country back in the sixties when blacks looted stores, burned buildings, and trashed the communities where they lived. Their actions were totally wrong, misplaced, and unproductive, but they seemed not to care. At that point, I began to understand the psychology of the human mind when someone feels oppressed and under duress. Again, I am not trying to excuse or justify what I did or what was done in the sixties but suggest that I understood why I did what I did and treated it as a learning experience so that it would never happen again. Suffice to say, all of us were sent to be reprimanded for our actions through a formal hearing, or what the navy calls an executive mass.

This was my first offense, and I had never come close to committing such an act. We were summoned separately; therefore, I can't speak to what happened to the other guys. At the hearing, I recall giving an honest appeal of why I did what I did and how I felt at that moment. Frustration was the only word I could think of as I explained that my behavior was out of character. I told him, because of my frustration, I simply didn't think or care about the consequences of my actions. I had no rational, conscious thoughts because things appeared hopeless, especially considering my basic training experience. I explained how my aspirations of playing with the navy band were crushed when I didn't pass my final audition. I had almost given up my dream of playing music. I spoke mainly about my feelings and did not focus on any resentments. As I recall, I asked one pointed question to the examiner in my hearing. The question was, "How would you feel and what would you do if you were in my shoes?" I don't quite remember his response, but nearly two weeks later, I received my orders for my next duty station. I believe I was fortunate in this regard because I was only reprimanded verbally, and my actions had not jeopardized my future in the military. The others who were party to our outbursts and disregard of civility were still at the camp when I left.

Returning home, for the first time after nearly six months in boot camp, was refreshing, and I hoped for a new start in my military service. I was home for only one week before I was approached by my sister and cousins who wanted to drive to Chicago and stay the weekend to see Johnny Taylor, a popular artist, perform on a Friday night at a famous club. Neither of them had a driver's license, and they convinced me to drive because I had one. Our trip to Chicago was short and uneventful. After reaching Chicago, about 289 miles just northeast of St. Louis, we joined other family members, one being a cousin, the late Betty Everett, a popular soul singer and pianist in the sixties and early seventies who made hits like "There'll Come a Time" and "You're No Good," probably best known for her biggest hit single, the "Shoop Shoop Song" or "It's in His Kiss." Even though I had just left the vicinity of Chicago, with reluctance, I said I would go mainly because I had not seen Betty in a while and didn't want to disappoint my sister and cousins.

The night before we planned to leave Chicago, we went to another cousin's home. That night, I climbed on my cousin's motorbike a little inebriated and nearly killed myself. It was dark that night with few streetlights as I began my journey down what appeared to be a bumpy road. For some reason, I lost control, and as I did, I increased my speed to maintain balance, but the bike threw me off, and I nearly cut half the heel of my left foot. That experience of course ended my trip to Chicago, and I returned home on a plane because I couldn't drive back to St. Louis. My injury resulted in nearly fifteen stitches, and my mobility was assisted by crutches for about three months before I could walk on my own.

# Seas of Paralysis with Favor

The incident was bad timing because my new duty station would be on a ship. Due to my injury, I received light duty, and with the help and support from shipmates, I was able to get around the ship adequately. This was a side shot to my pride, ego, and independent nature because I hated having to depend on anyone. The ship's permanent station was in Norfolk, Virginia, but when I first boarded, it was docked in Berkley, Virginia, awaiting repairs before leaving for another Mediterranean cruise. By the time I was able to walk without crutches, the ship had been repaired and moved back to Norfolk. The ship was called the USS *Arcturus*, a small freighter or cargo ship that was relatively old and frequently required repairs. The ship's primary mission was to replenish other navy vessels such as large supply ships and aircraft carriers. My ship was small and had only about three hundred crew members, including a few commissioned officers. For comparison, in size, an aircraft carrier has about five thousand navy personnel aboard the ship.

Prior to departing for my first ship's cruise, I was taken off light duty and received duties as an onboard seaman. I worked directly under the supervision of the ship's boatswain mate who was in charge of maintaining the external structure of the ship. I was immediately assigned to work as one of the deck's crew who cleaned, painted, swept, and carried out other maintenance work such as rigging, loading, and unloading cargo. This was physical work I had not signed up for, and it was difficult for me to imagine I would be doing this kind of work over the next three and a half years. While in port, we would work from sunup to sundown with a supervisor continually standing over us, watching as if we could not be trusted to work hard. After six months of living on the ship, I had become despondent and felt dejected and discouraged by my circumstances. After the ship left port for my first Mediterranean cruise, the loneliness I felt many times before returned to my consciousness, and I wondered if I had made the biggest mistake of my life by joining the navy. The thought plagued me for a long time, especially while at sea because I had a lot of time to think. The ship would take, on average, ten days to reach its destination. While at sea, part of my duties included standing watch for four hours within a twenty-four-hour cycle to observe ocean contacts. This duty involved standing watch on the bridge, bow, fantail, port, and starboard sides of the ship, looking for vessels within an approximate twelve-mile radius with an objective of reporting contact coordinates back to the captain on the bridge. Standing watch was probably the most exhausting and dangerous experience at sea. Each time the ship sailed, it encountered storms that sent water to the highest levels of the ship. I would stand watch night and day during the cruise, and the worst part was at night when everyone else was sleeping. These were times when I felt afraid and the loneliest.

Another disheartening part of being a deckhand was that we would usually be kept on the ship working longer while other crew members were the first to enjoy time off the ship. The ship would spend three months in port and three months away. While cruising, we would frequently replenish other vessels that experienced six to nine months at sea. On the bright side, our ship would reach our destination and dock at several overseas ports such as Spain, Italy, France, and Greece where we were given generous liberties to explore different sites in these countries. Exploring the sites of these countries was the highlight of my navy tour. From this vantage, I got to see and experience places I would have never seen had I not signed up for the navy.

While aboard the ship, I met some very good people and became good friends to many of my shipmates. We were a very tight crew. We worked, played, and laughed together. We enjoyed each other's company whether on or off the ship. We had many bad, good, and sad experiences during the nearly two years while I was aboard the ship. I witnessed shipmates being court martialed, promoted to higher ranks, and one particular shipmate die from a car accident while on liberty. My shipmates called me "Wash" and the cleanup man because I was always the one who tried to make peace when someone made trouble. I was the first to clean up a mess if our backs were against the wall, on or off the ship. Although I disliked the functions of my ship duties, I worked hard and did the best job I could. I was commended, on several occasions, on how well I performed the task given me and constantly encouraged by my superiors to work toward becoming a boatswain's mate. However, I just couldn't put my mind around serving in that capacity for the rest of my navy tour, and I resisted their offers.

After about a year on the ship, an opportunity was presented to deck seamen to apply for a gunner's mate apprentice position. Considering how I felt about working on the deck and other components of my job, I jumped at the opportunity and applied for this position, as did many others. For a reason unknown to me, I was chosen for the job, which was, under the circumstances, the best job I could have been given while aboard that particular ship. The ship's gunnery division was very small and had only two members, myself and a second-class petty officer gunner's mate who supervised me. Unlike working on the deck with supervisor boatswain mates watching my every move, he was very relaxed and seldom around to constantly monitor my work. My workload was light, and my duties were to primarily maintain the armory's weaponry. The armory was only equipped with several M1/ M16 rifles, many .45-caliber pistols, and associated paraphernalia. As a result of this job, I became an expert at disassembling, cleaning, and reassembling the firearms aboard the ship.

The gunnery position allowed me to have more freedom than I could have ever imagined. During spare time, I was able to walk around the ship and visit other shipmates while they were busy doing their jobs. I enjoyed this job so well that I seriously considered becoming a gunner's mate, so I began studying and preparing for the test. If passed, I would become a gunner's mate, third-class petty officer, which is the next step up from seaman apprentice. However, prior to committing myself by taking the test, rumors began to float around that the ship was slated to be decommissioned. The rumors were true in short time, and the ship's crew began the decommissioning process. With this news came along the fact that shipmates, if not discharged, would be transferred to a different duty station. I for one, had to make an important decision, because I was seriously considering a gunner's mate position on this particular ship but reticent about being placed on another ship, because gunner's mates only served on ships. Prior to my decision to taking the test, I received new orders for shore duty in New York City. After receiving the orders, it was obvious to me what I would do. I decided to accept the orders to avoid being placed on another ship. Although I enjoyed the idea of traveling, I had become tired of the confined quarters on a ship.

Preparing for decommission was grueling and involved much physical work for crew members. This was one case where everyone pitched in to prepare the ship for decommissioning regardless of title or rank. It took a couple months to complete this task. I recall working in the bowels of the ship's portholes where I and others chipped paint for hours at a time before taking a break. It was a daunting and fainthearted experience crawling through long tunnels no more than two feet high and three feet wide, chipping paint from the walls with electric drill handguns and very little lighting. While performing these jobs, all of the crew lived off the ship in a barracks nearby. Once the job was completed, it was time for each of us to leave and report to our next assigned duty station. Bidding farewell to shipmates was sobering and a little sad because most of us had lived together for nearly two years. I had developed friendships with many of the crew but had to accept going our separate ways. We had not only worked together but had spent much of our pastime relaxing, eating, partying, and frolicking, which made life bearable on the ship. I had met many good men whom I became very close to but unfortunately loss contact with them after leaving for New York City.

## Mixed Bag of Glitter and Illusion

To be honest, I was ready for a change and looked forward to a new adventure while contemplating a new chapter in my life to complete my last two years in the navy on land. When I arrived in New York City in 1973, there would remain many bumps in the road as I adjusted to everyday circumstances. I was stationed in Brooklyn, New York, and lived on the base where everything I needed was conveniently inside one huge structure. The building had a commissary, administrative office, and living quarters for navy personnel. Living in a building having the many activities and comforts of home without having to leave the building was a tremendous asset. For extracurricular activities, the building had a nightclub, movie theater, cafeteria, commissary, and pool hall. There were many military personnel and civilian employees who worked in the building. My passion for music never ended, and I took advantage of playing my sax every chance I got. The nightclub in the building was frequented by military members as well as civilians. The club would hire a popular band to entertain audiences once a week. I would occasionally ask if I could sit in for a few songs, and they would oblige. I became very popular and a known musician. The pool hall, located on the ground floor of the building, was large with eight standard pool tables. During my leisure, I would practice every day playing pool. The club also had a pool table, a little smaller than the pool hall but one that attracted many excellent pool players. I was seldom beaten in pool and was known as one of the best pool players in the building.

The sweet part of my experience was that I was very popular in the building and seemingly began to attract people

I had never thought of meeting. Although motivations were different, there were many men and women who approached me, without my reaching out, for friendship. It was like having won a lottery of some kind with everyone wanting a part of you. This was certainly a new experience for me, and I enjoyed the attention.

When I first arrived at my new duty station to set up my stay, I was sent to the third floor of the building, where living and sleeping quarters included a long hall with twenty open cubicles similar to the temporary barracks I lived in during my ship's decommissioning preparation. I thought it was a little odd that I would be sharing living quarters with such little privacy considering I was stationed there for the next two years. The open cubicles were small with a twin-sized bed, two wood framed compartments for clothes, and a few other accessories. This was certainly not what I thought my living conditions would be, but because of my unquestioning naivety and the fact it was my permanent duty station, I accepted and adapted to the new provisions given me. This didn't bother me as much because I had been accustomed to close living quarters. I got to know and became acquainted with many who lived on that particular floor.

Many of them, like myself, had no formal education and were a little rough around the edges, but they had plenty of street smarts. The building also housed a marine brig located on the top floor of the building, specifically set aside for truant navy personnel, but I did not immediately make the connection that most of them left the brig before being moved to the floor I was living on. What I later realized was that most of them were simply transients waiting to be discharged under unfavorable conditions because they had flagrantly abused navy policy in some way. Most transients who left the brig would only have about a month or two before being discharged. As months passed, more transients would leave the brig and move onto the floor, where they remained until they were discharged, but they still had the freedom to move about the building with little monitoring. Many continued to approach me for their friendship based on my popularity and what they thought they could gain by befriending me.

Several months passed before I realized I should have been provided a room instead of living like a transient passing through waiting for discharge papers. Until then, most of my closest associates were those who lived in those close quarters and who meant no good to anyone. Over time, my eyes were opened to the fact that those individuals were only looking for trouble, and it became clear they did not have the best intentions for me or anyone else. After speaking to a high-ranking navy officer and sharing my living conditions, I discovered I should have been provided private living quarters. He was shocked to find out I had been living on the same floor and sharing space with navy personnel who were essentially being discharged from the navy for various unsavory reasons. He made it clear to me that he would do what he could to set things straight and right the wrong. Shortly after our conversation, I was placed in a room that accommodated two people. The new living quarters were perfect and just what I needed.

## Apple of Delight

Living on base was my first New York experience, and I had no clue as to what would follow once I became familiar with the town. After I began to get out and enjoy the city of New York, I realized how much I had to learn about the fast life. People in New York were cordial but very direct in their behavior and attitudes. New York was a city with virtually everything you could name; if New York doesn't have it, it doesn't exist. New York City is comprised of five boroughs— Brooklyn, Queens, Staten Island, the Bronx, and Manhattan where most of the commerce and nightlife occurs. Nearly eight million people were packed into the five boroughs of New York City, with Brooklyn being the largest borough. Brooklyn had about three million people alone and would be considered one of the largest cities in the nation if it were a city. It took me nearly a year to learn and adapt to the culture and pace of New York City. When I started driving in New York, I was astonished by the lack of courtesy. Drivers were very aggressive, would not think twice about cutting you off, and wouldn't yield even slightly. However, after a few months, I fit right in.

I recall my first visit to Manhattan, a fabulous metropolis for dining, shopping, and partying. Seeing the tall skyscrapers, bright lights, and huge visual displays of various advertisements was especially exciting. The first time I'd ever seen the homeless was when visiting Manhattan. Of course, it had much more to offer than a few individuals who needed help. There was a plethora of things to do and enjoy. There were Broadway shows, glamorous stores to shop in, nightclubs, bars, restaurants, and much more entertainment. It was a rich experience exploring Manhattan, especially for the first time.

## Job to Nowhere

I was assigned to a unit called Commander Eastern Sea Frontier located nearly a short block away on the same street where I lived. The office where I worked had mostly commissioned officers. The office included three other enlisted personnel besides myself, two yeomen, second- and first-class petty officers, and one chief petty officer who all served administrative duties. The building where I worked also included many civilian workers who supported navy operations. As a seaman, I arrived as the lowest-ranking member of that particular office unit. My job was to carry confidential and other pertinent documents to the admiral who conducted his work from the United Nations (UN) building. I drove and carried materials twice a day, in the morning and afternoon. Between my morning and afternoon trips, I worked on the admiral's barge alongside a second-class boatswain's mate, but for some reason, I very seldom had to work on the barge. My overall job wasn't a glamorous one, but I didn't mind because it had its perks. The advantages included wearing a suit every day and being provided a black sedan to drive while on and sometimes off duty. Wearing a suit was attractive to others, and I felt special because most navy personnel had to wear their regular uniforms while on duty. I was given a government credit card specifically for gas. I could also use a navy fuel pump located on site for navy vehicles. Of course with these privileges came certain responsibilities that I at first took seriously but over time took advantage of, and I became sometimes irresponsible.

Having this particular job was great in the beginning but yielded trouble for me later on. After about eight months of driving back and forth to the UN, I became a little despondent because when I looked back over the past three years in the navy, I had accomplished very little. I began, again, to think about why I joined the navy and how things actually turned out for me. I was not pleased and decided to speak with the ranking officer I had spoken to earlier about my navy experiences and how my plans failed. I told him that my primary reason for joining the navy was to be a musician, but it didn't work out. I told him about my basic training experience, which included being placed in a holding company while waiting two and a half months before receiving my deserved two weeks' leave. He was a good listener, and after hearing all my woes, he asked what I would like to do for the remainder of my navy term. To be honest, I had not thought that far ahead. The same officer suggested I seek out other opportunities within the office where I worked. I was only a seamen up to that point. The next step higher would be a third-class petty officer. I spoke with the chief yeoman at the time, and he said he would support my efforts to become a yeoman, if I were interested. The yeoman position served as administrative support function for the office and required being able to type thirty words a minute, minimum. I had never typed a day in my life. The chief provided me with a manual typewriter, and I taught myself how to type. It took a couple of months before I was able to reach the navy's required proficiency to become a yeoman. I also had to study and pass a basic military requirement test. I studied hard and subsequently passed the test, and to my surprise, with flying colors. After taking the test, I was told I nearly aced the test, and I became a ranking yeoman third-class petty officer for the United States Navy. This was one of my few accomplishments, considering I was on my way out after two and a half years of enlisted service.

# Taste of Ambivalent Thoughts

From the beginning of my arrival to my new duty station in New York, my guard was up, and shortly afterwards, I became very skeptical of those with whom I associated. It appeared to me that everyone I met, especially the men who lived on the same floor as I, had ulterior motives or a hidden agenda for everything they did.

I felt as if people thought I had a hidden chest of valuable jewels waiting to share with whoever had the most convincing story to tell about their needs. I was very popular and had need for nothing except to have friends and be happy. At the same time, I preserved my thoughts and became very suspicious in all my dealings with people. Although I dealt with probably hundreds of folks, I didn't allow many to get too close. Maybe I led people to believe I had a lot to offer, but deep inside I was insecure and troubled. There may have been a few who were genuine with respect to having sincere motives, but I was very protective of myself. Almost everyone I met seemed to have their hands out wanting something and willing to give back very little in return. Even with my popularity, I was perplexed about many things and ambivalent about not being able to develop genuine relationships with others.

There were brief moments of paranoia where I thought people were plotting against me even though I had no proof or evidence to support it. In reality, people were just being people, some operating from selfishness, some being deceitful, and some having honorable intensions. Over time, I realized it was my inner soul looking for truth to fill a void. During this period of my life, my mind was fraught with distrust and disillusionment with human behavior, including my own. As my sensibility of sadness, disappointment, and distrust began to flow through my consciousness, I was reminded of my Christian roots. Even with those guided principles with which I identified, I thought about all of the past mistakes I had made and the mental anguish it brought. I thought about the pain, agony, and hardships I endured over the years because of my sometimes-aberrant conduct. I also considered my humane acts of kindness and desire to treat people as I wanted to be treated, which brought me peace and comforted my soul.

It was at this point when I began to examine my life and reconsider my walk with Christ. I wasn't quite ready to act on this notion, but I gave it considerable thought. It wasn't until I met a bodybuilder who was thinking the same way I did. He and I became good friends, and we influenced each other to make a commitment to attend church. We were certainly on the same page. As we talked about our past and how we felt about our individual situations, we decided to start a new beginning by serving God, who we believed, at that time, was our only refuge. Although we lost contact over the years, I still consider him one of my best friends. His name is Dudley Green.

## Reconciling Mistakes with Truth

There were several mistakes I made before I was discharged, and I paid a heavy price for making them. One big mistake I made was initially small to me but came back to slap me in the face. I let someone I barely knew use the government gas credit card and forgot over time that I did. This person was apparently struggling financially, and I decided to help by letting him use the gas credit card issued by the government to me and for my use only. I knew at the time it was the wrong thing to do, but wanting to help, I ignored my common sense and personal responsibility for safeguarding government property and gave the credit card to him to use. My rationale for allowing him to use the credit card was that I had access to a government gas pump at any time and that I didn't need the card. The problem was that I allowed him to use the card in the first place, and in addition, he was one of the transients I knew. At the time, I had no reason to think he would not give it back because we all lived on the same base. I know it was irresponsible, but I did it anyway, which clearly indicates my frame of mind at that moment. However, he was actually discharged and never returned. Obviously, the credit card was not returned, and over time, I simply forgot I had loaned it to him because I didn't really need it. It never crossed my mind that anything would come from the fact that I had abused a privilege of handling government property. It never dawned on me that something could happen to the card and ultimately I would be made responsible for my lack of judgment. Several months had passed before being summoned to an Agency of Investigations for questioning. I had no idea why I was called to report there, and I went ready and willingly to answer any questions put before me. The first question before me was not particularly threatening because the individual they asked if I knew was nonexistent to me at the time asked. In my mind, the name mentioned was someone I thought I didn't know. So I told them I did not know this individual. But after further questioning, I vaguely remembered the name because they brought up the government credit card. Then it became uncomfortable because I didn't really want to deliberately lie. The next question was more pointed. "Do you have the government's gas credit card given to you when you were provided the government's vehicle?" This question tested my inner consciousness of morality because I knew the answer and immediately remembered that I did once have the government's credit card. Just as the answer raced through my mind, in a split second, I remembered that I had allowed someone to use the card but never got it back, although I didn't remember his name. By this time, I knew exactly where the inquiry was headed. My second answer was yes without an explanation. But as I waited for the next question, the thought raced through my mind that I was in big trouble and whether or not I should continue to be honest in my responses. I knew what I had done was wrong, and now it had caught up to me. I was then asked if I still had the credit card, and my answer was no, again without an explanation. The follow-up question was, "What happened to the credit card?" and my answer was I didn't know, which was vague but not totally true. I didn't know where the credit card was, but I surely remembered, by now, I had allowed someone to use it, and it was never returned to me. Apparently, the individual had used the credit card repeatedly until he got caught. Again, the thought of whether or not I should be truthful raced through my mind because I could anticipate the next question. I could easily say I lost the card a long time ago but didn't think to report it because I didn't need it. The next question was, "Did you loan the credit card to someone for their personal use?" At this time in my life, I had begun to turn to God for my help and deliverance. Thus, I needed to be responsible, to own and acknowledge my wrong, and I did. There was no other need for discussion because I admitted what I had done. The next step was to accept the consequences to come. I went before an admiral, a four-star flag officer of the navy, and he gave me the works. My penalty for the abuse was probably fair but appeared to be extreme to me because I was busted back to seaman and suffered a monthly fine for three consecutive months. The magnitude of this judgment was particularly huge to me because I had worked so hard to obtain the petty officer stripe, and it was taken away with a word and a pen. At that time, I had about eight months left in the navy. I considered the possibility that after four years in the military, I would be discharged with only an E3 rating, which is the rating you automatically receive after basic training. A reasonable and attainable rank after four years was probably an E6. I felt like a complete failure, and once again, I reflected on the time of my enlistment and how things did not work out for me in basic training. If I had not trusted in God, my mind would have stayed in a space where I would not have wanted it to be. But I was at peace with the decision and consequence, which I deserved.

The positive side of this ordeal was the fact that the captain in my office approached me and promised to do his best for me to regain my petty officer stripe before I was discharged. He stated he couldn't do much about the financial part of my judgment, but he would work toward restoring my rank. About six months before I was discharged from the navy, I got my third-class petty officer stripe back. I was very grateful for what the captain did and thankful that he was led by the kindness of his heart to intervene for me. I left the navy in 1975 with an honorable discharge as yeoman third-class petty officer. After my discharge, I decided to remain in New York instead of returning to St. Louis where I grew up. My navy tour proved to be bittersweet and, in retrospect, played a major role in making me who I am today even with all the pieces. I am certainly gratified to have served in the military and proud to be a navy veteran.

# CHAPTER 8
• • • • • • • • • • •
## Marriage with Peace and Pieces

Peace, in many instances, is entangled with the pieces of living, and marriage is no exception. Getting married and vowing to share a life with someone is an undertaking many appear to take lightly. This venture should be weighed carefully and thoughtfully before the commitment is made because it is not only the words you say during the marriage ceremony but, more importantly, the actual deeds that follow. It's very easy to say, "I do," but it is not easy to obligate yourself to someone else for a lifetime. With any marriage, short or long in duration, there will be times of troubles and times of fulfillment. The troubles will come sooner than later, which may involve unanticipated predicaments arising in many forms, such as hardships, difficulties, afflictions, and pain. Marriage can also bring happiness, joy, peace, comfort, satisfaction, solace, and security. Both the troubles and fulfillment in our marriage are inevitable occurrences of life. However, finding the key to having peace while enduring these parallel essential forms of dichotomy seems to be elusive to most who enter into the terrestrial realm of matrimony. Unfortunately, too often, many marriages end in a divorce decree.

I met my then future wife at a local church in Harlem New York, one year prior to being discharged from the navy while stationed in Brooklyn, New York. I was in a whirl spin of mental anguish and needed deliverance from a pattern of doubt. I began attending the church and had just recommitted my life to Christ after wandering many years in the abyss of following my self-delusional efforts to make peace with everyone. I was discharged from the navy in 1975 and married my wife the same year to begin a journey together. I was twenty-three, and she was eighteen when we married. I believe both of us took our vows seriously to commit ourselves to each other for a lifetime. My wife and I have been married more than forty years, but we are no exception to the rule in that we started out loving each other with the idea to have the proverbial marital bliss. As newlyweds, it was nearly impossible to look upstream and see the troubles and heartaches we, as a couple, would face during the next ten, twenty, thirty, or more years. We were both young, naïve, and inexperienced to this new way of life but believed strongly, with God's help, we could endure the journey and withstand the challenges we would face. As with all couples, there will be mistakes made, disagreements, and disappointments, and sometimes even distrust will develop when least expected. I brought to the marriage my own personal baggage, expectations, and preconceived notions of living together as one. These are the beginning of any couple's woes, which can bring havoc to a marriage. My baggage included the impediments of the environment from which I was raised. The expectations and preconceptions were aligned with and founded by the ideals of how I envisioned our needs would be met by coming together as one. None of them were realistically conceived or taken into account. Instead, early on, our marriage became a learning ground of disappointment, disillusionment, and misplaced desires for self-gain, which marks an unpleasant beginning and weak foundation. But the rough spots in any marriage, just as with many other of life's lessons, help build individual character and manifest the most fulfilling enjoyments of living together.

My wife and I have seen the worst and the best of times. We have faced the trials of marital tribulation with dismay but have survived the storms of troubles, pain, hardships, and yes, even the self- afflicted marital discourse. From experience, I know these things will pass, only if you stay together and give the past time to heal. I have learned that marriage is not a fifty-

fifty proposition but requires both parties to give sacrificially, especially when one party falls short of his or her responsibilities. It is not easy and deserves more thought than most conceive when approaching the vows of matrimony. Sometimes one party may be required to give as much as 70 percent while the other languishes in misguided pursuits, whether it is through a betrayal of some kind, misfortunes, or sickness. But with time, and in most cases, the table will turn, and the other party will have to make the same kinds of adjustments and sacrifices.

My wife and I were blessed with three lovely daughters within the first four years of marriage, Sharmaine, Porsha, and Michelle. Living in New York City was a huge challenge with the cost of living so high and neither of us having the type of formal education to financially maintain a family of five. I had just started an entry-level job that salaried just slightly above minimum wage. My wife stayed home to take care of our kids and, to be candid, was the pillar of our family structure. I struggled for several years just trying to make ends meet financially, and with that came hardship and discomfort. During this period was stress and tension because I simply was not equipped mentally or financially to provide the proper stability for a growing family. There were times of discontentment for me because I felt unprepared to provide for my family adequately. I was young and didn't have the maturity or wisdom to raise a family, and I made mistakes. There were times, strictly due to my behavior, when my wife had reservations about my obligation to her and our marriage vows. She would catch me looking at other women, and the distrust became so profound it could have ended if she had not taken seriously her commitment to the marriage.

Although things were hard, I believe I did the best I could and managed to survive financially with the help, occasionally, from family and friends. The support we got, especially when the chips were down, was not taken lightly. When we were first married, I did not have a car, but the beneficent help from many friends made life much more bearable. Several of our friends would, at certain intervals, drive us were we needed to go. Driving our entire family to church was especially a big deal. Later in marriage, our financial situation improved considerably. I had completed college, my income more than quadrupled and, my wife had already started pursuing higher education.

Although we were financially stable, we were still treading through hard knocks of marital discourse. We disagreed on many things. For instance, we had different ideas on how to raise our kids and how to manage our financial resources, including the right versus wrong choices we both made, all of which caused strain and forms of anxiety in our marriage. As with most things, these got better, and we were able to rise above the sometimes-petty discord. By this time, my wife was working, and our combined income was well over six figures, placing us in the middle to upper income tax brackets. We were financially stable, had grown, had developed enough faith in one another, and were satisfied with the true commitment we had vowed to keep when we were first married. Even during this period, there were still periods of stress and the weight of unfulfilled expectations we both carried.

When we reached our thirtieth anniversary, we officially renewed our wedding vows to show the commitment we had developed for each other. We had been through so many trials together and had passed so many hurdles; it was unimaginable to think differently. At this juncture in our marriage, the thought of not being married was beyond the thought of our consciousness. By the time we reached forty years of marriage, the vows we took, "to death do us part," had become synonymous with our actions and deeds. We had gained maturity and wisdom, neither of which comes easy without first living in pieces.

There is much to be said about a wife and mother. My wife deserves probably more than she realizes. She continues to bring an abundance of stability to our marriage. She has played a huge role in solidifying our marriage for all of these years and is always the one to offer the practical solutions to problems we face. I don't mean to down play my part in the marriage, because I have contributed immensely to our successful marriage resolve. Both of us have managed to live with a modicum of peace while enduring the pieces of life thrown our way. My wife is a solid rock of greatness and my best friend. Without her in my life, I would be like a bird with broken wings. My wife's name is Dr. Glenda Washington.

# CHAPTER 9
## Unobstructed Peace

My MOTHER-IN-LAW PLAYED AN IMPORTANT role in my life, which allowed me to know myself better. Prior to marrying my wife and meeting her mother was an experience I never expected. When I was first introduced to my wife's mother, unlike her father, her mother appeared to be cold, unimpressed by my appearance, and disappointed that her daughter would date someone like me, especially taking into account our age difference. I am five and a half years older than my wife, and her mother didn't like the idea of her daughter seriously dating someone my age and being so young. My wife had not graduated high school, and the possibility of interrupting her future college aspirations seemed to have been even more troubling to my wife's mother. She was certainly unimpressed because I was still in the military and I did not have definitive career goals at that time. I surmise I appeared to be just another young black man from the streets of New York. To further complicate matters, her daughter and I had become serious about our relationship. In retrospect and considering these factors, I really can't blame my mother-in-law's first impression and initial response when we first met.

I met my wife's father first but under completely different circumstances. I attended and became a church member where he, his son, and two daughters were members. Her father's son was about a year older than my future wife, and the other daughter was a couple years younger. His daughter, my future wife, was seventeen, and I was twenty-two when we actually first met. The age difference between his daughter and I had already been settled in his mind, and we had developed a cordial relationship well before his daughter and I began courting, which made a big difference in his attitude. Her father had also watched me closely and was aware of my commitment to and faith in God, as well as the seriousness I had concerning my Christian walk. As with any father, he had initial concerns whether or not his daughter, who had not graduated high school, was making a wise decision jumping into a serious relationship so soon. However, the fact our church's pastor had sanctioned the relationship between his daughter and me made it easier for him to accept.

My, then future mother-in-law never attended the church and had not been given the opportunity to know me as well as my future father-in-law. By the time we were introduced, her daughter and I had already begun to date and had formed the beginnings of a serious relationship. Again, this fact was very disturbing to the mother. She had high hopes for her daughter's future and felt our relationship would prevent her daughter from completing college, as did her oldest daughter who studied medicine and became a medical doctor. I got the sense that the mother's hopes and dreams she had for her daughter's career were going up in smoke, based on this one decision. At the time, I believed she thought her daughter was making a big mistake by courting someone like me, considering the fact I had no formal education and limited future plans. I didn't at the time and could not blame her for thinking the way she did. I knew she was simply a concerned parent who had her daughter's best interest at heart. The fact that her husband was on board with their daughter starting a budding relationship at her age made the situation more problematic for her. The mother's disapproval and disappointment seemed to have put distance between her daughter as well as her husband, which I believe made it more difficult for her to embrace, accept, or even acknowledge this reality.

I didn't realize how much my wife's mother was against

our relationship until our wedding day. She did not attend our wedding, and she and her daughter rarely spoke to one another afterwards for some time. To say the least, I felt slightly guilty because of my wife and her mother's strained relationship and ambivalent because I loved my wife and wanted the approval from her mother. Because of the tension between the two, I believed, at the time, her mother not attending our wedding meant more to my wife than she was willing to admit, but I later realized their relationship had been strained before we met.

After our wedding, several months passed, and my wife's mother appeared to be more receptive to the idea we were married. Proof of this was when her mother gave us a late wedding gift of several hundred dollars, which was plenty back in those days. We certainly could use the money, and it came in handy as struggling newlyweds. My mother-in-law appeared to be much harder on my wife than any of her other five siblings, and I really could not understand why because my wife seemed to be the most compliant sibling to me. For several years, there appeared to me much tension between them, and of course, I believed it was because of me but later realized it was far deeper than I had imagined. As with many relationships, with time, people began to soften up, giving time for wounds to heal and allowing reconciliation to take hold. This appeared to have been the case with the relationship between my wife and her mother, which improved considerably overtime.

I believed my mother-in-law loved her daughter, just as I knew my wife loved her mother, notwithstanding the tension and sometimes distrust between the two. My mother-in-law was a strict disciplinarian and very outspoken in how she felt. She would say what she meant and meant what she said. That's not all bad because I always knew what was on her mind, and she never spoke in uncertain terms. She was transparent in all her ways, and I don't believe she meant harm to anyone. Considering her mother's frankness, I could see how easy it was for her to be misunderstood. Regardless, I always felt she was a good person who simply viewed the world only through a black or white lens.

## Double Indemnity

During this period, plans for my future still included getting a college education but would not be actualized until after I completed the four years of military service. After leaving the navy and working for a couple years, I enrolled in York College of the University of New York. By then, I was married and had two little girls, which did not deter me from making this important decision. At the time, I was employed by the weather service, working forty hours a week while I attended York. After the first couple years at York, while studying geology, I enrolled in City College of the University of New York to also study meteorology. I simultaneously attended both colleges while carrying twelve credits per semester and working full-time. My plans were always to study meteorology, but I entered York because the campus was close to where I lived at the time, located in Jamaica Queens, New York. I was fully aware that York College did not offer a curriculum in meteorology, but, for convenience sake, I decided to attend York first, transfer to City College after two years, and declare a major in meteorology. At the end of two years, I had already satisfied all my electives, invested time at York, and acquired credits in geology. That being the case, I decided to pursue the two majors. The fact that York College and City College were part of the City University of New York (CUNY) network, I made the decision to attend both simultaneously. My studies in these majors were completed in 1983.

As a reflection point, I endured six years attending college, working full-time while carrying twelve credits per semester. I got very little sleep while supporting a wife and three young children. I wanted to quit school on several occasions, especially when I failed and had to repeat classes in physics and calculus, two core requirements for both major studies. This piece of my life was extremely exhaustive, and I sometimes felt defeated, but I vowed that I would never quit because I knew my future was at stake. I persevered and accomplished what I had set out to do by completing two important scientific studies.

Shortly after graduating college, I received a scholarship through my job to attend the University of Wisconsin. I was one of six participants chosen with math or science degrees to receive the scholarship and granted full tuition and other expenses through a graduate scientist program, which concluded after fifteen months. This opportunity was presented at the right time because I had become consciously fatigued from the past grueling six years while working and undertaking undergraduate studies.

Completing college was certainly a highlight of my life's journey and a memorable accomplishment, especially considering my circumstances and the seemingly unabated pressure. During this piece of life, I gained great respect for education and profited from the academic knowledge acquired from this experiential voyage. Although slightly turbulent, it was a peaceful adventure.

# Peace by Choice

Many years passed, and I completed college in 1983. I rarely encountered my mother-in-law's wrath because I hardly saw her. Even when I did, my attitude toward her was always cordial despite her frankness, and I had the utmost respect for her simply because she was my wife's mother, and that's what she deserved. In my humble opinion, she was no different from most of us who hold the baggage and vestiges of our upbringing and personal experiences, carrying them like a cloud that never goes away. Quite frankly, my behavior toward my mother- in-law was no different from my behavior toward my own mother, who seemed to be overbearing at times but whom I loved.

As mentioned, shortly after graduating college, I received an opportunity of a lifetime. I was granted a scholarship, with all expenses paid, to attend and study meteorology at the University of Wisconsin. My wife and I had three little girls, ages seven, five, and four. After accepting the offer, we decided all of us would go live in Wisconsin and return home after I completed my studies.

We had recently purchased a home, which neither of us wanted to sell. Prior to this, my wife's father and mother had divorced, and her mother lived alone in an apartment. The thought of her moving into our home until we returned was a big consideration. By this time, the relationship between my wife and her mother had improved considerably, and I certainly did not have any objection to her mother staying in our home until we returned. When we approached my mother-in-law, she was amenable to the idea and graciously accepted our request to take care of our home while we were away. My wife and I, of course, agreed to continue paying the mortgage and other expenses to maintain the property.

We lived in Madison, Wisconsin, which is considered a college town, and we enjoyed every bit of it. Life in Madison was very easygoing, attractive, and inviting, a noticeable contrast to the alluring excitement, huge population, and fast-paced environment of New York City. During the fifteen months living in Madison, we developed many relationships. A few distant family members also lived in Beloit, Wisconsin, about fifty miles west of Madison, which added to our pleasant stay. We would visit them during my semester breaks. New York is a great place to live and has everything any other place can offer; however, after enjoying the neighborly Wisconsin experience and retuning to the congestive traffic, potholes, population density, and the city's fast pace, we knew then that if an opportunity came along to move, we would probably not hesitate.

## Showing Honor and Respect

When we got back to New York and arrived home during the summer of 1984, we both immediately knew that it would be unfair and inconsiderate to tell my wife's mother she had to move. We only had three bedrooms, but the kids were still young enough to share a bedroom, and we allowed her mother to stay. As our kids got a little older and bigger, things were getting pretty crowded in our home, but my wife and I, still wanting her mother to stay, had to come up with a plan. We considered the unfinished basement, which no one used, and decided to fix it up, allowing her mother to live there. We had the basement finished by hiring a contractor to include two bedrooms, a kitchen, bathroom, and dining room, where her mother would have lots of space and the privacy she deserved. Her mother was no different from how she had been before we got married. Her words were still stinging, and her tone was still somewhat abrasive. One of my first mistakes with my mother-in-law was to address her by her first name. She was very direct and forceful in her tone that I should not call her by her first name. I was about twenty-four years old but didn't see any harm in calling her by her first name because, growing up, neither me nor many of my siblings addressed my mother as mom, and it was normal to call her by a nickname given to us. It was certainly not out of disrespect but a household culture from my upbringing.

However, apparently, in her mother's mind, I was being disrespectful, but I didn't mean any disrespect. I completely understood were she was coming from, and I had no problem conceding her request. I immediately began calling her Ms. G, which was okay with her. My mother would have never allowed me or my siblings to disrespect her in any way, and we knew better. Even after getting past that hurdle, my mother-in-law said many hurtful things to me, but I never believed her words were meant to be hurtful. She would seem to speak without filtering her words, and when she spoke, she spoke in very direct terms.

For example, my parents and other siblings from out of town would visit our home in New York from time to time. I recall when one of my younger sisters came to visit us for her first time, my mother-in-law, seemingly without forethought, uttered words I never thought would come from her lips, but they did. When they first met, the first words uttered from my mother-in-law's mouth were, "This is your sister? What happened to you?" To me, those were hurtful, piercing words and possessed a biting edge of sarcasm and disbelief. Her words were not easy to accept, but I bit my tongue and dismissed what she said without incident. My sister happens to have a light complexion, as do my mother and one other sister. The rest of us have dark complexions. In my own thoughtful way, I didn't give her words much further thought because I didn't think she meant any harm. Even if she did, I refused to dwell on something I could not control. I seemed to keep my peace that way.

  This was not the first time she made such statements, and I didn't think it would be the last. Her words seemed to never provoke me to anger. I did not take her words personally, and I very rarely do under similar circumstances. I also believe that some people, through their own broken spirit, say many things without realizing the hurt it can cause. Not to be psychoanalytical, but I think some people who lack this kind of sensitivity have usually suffered through years of inner discontentment of some kind. It was clear to me that even her behavior was no different from what is manifested by many. Although I was the target of my mother-in-law's seemingly constant indifference to how I felt, my life experiences, through human interaction, had taught me I have no control over what people say or what they do. I have always felt that love, understanding, and compassion can be a big influence over others, especially over time. Some people in my position would probably have developed resentment of some kind, but I chose not to.

# Change of Heart

Several years passed, and my mother-in-law suddenly surprised me when she apologized for her past derisive behavior and condemnation of me, especially for her conduct and attitude when we were first introduced. She further stated she had mistakenly misjudged me and regretted all the derogative things she said to me that were untrue and not thoughtful. She really touched my heart when she stated she considered me to be her best son-in-law and she had grown to love and see me as a respectable person. It was very sobering to hear her say those words and to witness her genuine change of heart. It was truly a reconciliation of the minds, which did not happen overnight but gradually through time. I can surmise the fruition of this encounter could have only come about through my consistent respect for her and by my overlooking her seemingly harsh disposition. It appears, without forethought, I have the propensity to give people the benefit of doubt even when their actions appear to be deliberate. No matter whom I encounter, I do my best to conduct my life in a way that conforms to love, civility, and respect. It may sound strange, but this attitude gives me peace of mind. It is ironic and remarkable that my mother-in-law lived within our household for more than ten years without incident before she moved back to Jamaica, her birthplace. This one particular experience epitomizes how I have conducted my life though living in peace while living in pieces. My mother-in-law passed a few years ago, and she left a legacy, in her own way, by raising six children who have done very well in their own rights and through their own individual accomplishments of growth and stability. I firmly believe she was a good mother to her children and raised them the best she could. She is missed by all of her family and friends. My wife's late mother's name is Gloria Walters. RIP.

# CHAPTER 10
## Interrupted Peace

My teenage years were filled with lots of interesting twists and turns but some interminable challenges. I was reliable, but as with many teens, I had irresponsible tendencies. Prior to college, there were several occasions when I certainly exhibited irresponsible behavior. One of these challenges was to deal with my guilt brought about when my son died. We all must confront the inevitable fact of life that we will die someday. And before we pass on, there may be many who die before we do. I have lived long enough to see grandparents, uncles, aunts, cousins, nephews, nieces, friends, and a host of others pass away. I loved them all and was sorry to see them go, but the death of my son impacted me more than any. My son's death invoked a heightened feeling of emotion I had never felt before. His death was devastating and brought about the most intensified feeling of guilt I've ever experienced. The reason for my guilt, I believe, is common to many young men like myself who walked down the path of being irresponsible and downright ignorant to the consequences that would follow those undesirable steps. My son's death interrupted my peace temporarily but also changed my way of thinking and gave me a different perspective on life. It wasn't that I did not already have a deep respect and love for people, but his death forced me to reconcile my internal struggles of being truly accountable for my actions. There were many missteps I took before my son's death. This particular error in my life began when I was about seventeen years old and became sexually active even when I knew better.

At the age of eighteen, I was promiscuous and got a young girl pregnant. She was only fifteen, and neither of us was prepared for the unfortunate predicament that would follow us for the rest of our lives. About six or seven months into her pregnancy, she told me I was the father, which I did not want to believe or accept. At the time, I had enrolled in and was about to attend college. I was numbed and afraid of the prospect of having a child this early in life and tried to convince myself that the yet unborn child could not be mine.

After leaving for college, I hurried to push the thought to the back of my mind but months later was told by my younger sister that the baby was born and he was a boy. My sister, who was a close friend to my son's mother, also told my mother. My mother called later and was curious why I had not told her I was responsible for a newborn child. My initial instinct was to convince her the baby was not mine, but I could not state definitively whether or not he was mine. I was simply uncommitted, and my response was neither to completely accept nor deny him being my son. I tried to be honest and simply replied that I was not sure if he was my child, knowing deep inside the possibility was very real.

I was a close friend to a brother of my son's mother. I grew up with him and knew very well. His family and mine had close ties. We all lived in the same neighborhood and attended elementary and high schools together. My relationship with her brother became strained, but we managed to maintain our friendship. By the time I spoke with my mom, my entire family was aware that I had a son, and all had instinctively welcomed him into our family. Being away from home helped me to concretely internalize the possibility still existed that he was not my son. However, my family did the opposite by treating him as family through gifts, babysitting, and inviting the mother and my son to family gatherings.

# Inhabitants of Denial

I attended Lane in the early seventies, only one semester before dropping out to enlist in the navy. The transition between leaving college and starting my military service was about two months and difficult to manage because I was able to see the little baby boy for the first time. He was born in 1970. When I returned home from school, I was caught between a rock and hard place because, on the one hand, I could not deny I had a son, and on the other, I didn't want to accept it. During this transition, I saw him for the first time when he was a few months old. My first encounter was very awkward because I had very little contact with his mother while away, and tension had begun to build not only between my son's mother and myself but between me and her family as well. My son's mother was living with her mother when I first saw him. I could not avoid the unpleasant feelings I had inside because of mixed emotions. I seemed to be accepting the fact he was my son, but up to that point, all my actions had been counterintuitive. The fact remained he was only a few months old when I saw him for the first time, and I had not actually spoken to his mother since leaving for college prior to my son's birth. This encounter was mentally exasperating and felt like a time warp. I felt bad because I knew I had been irresponsible, neglectful, and unaccountable for my behavior from the time she told me she was pregnant up to that point. The saving grace was the difference my family made, on my behalf, by accepting my son as family while I was away.

The fact there would be years before I actually felt any guilt was evident by my being in a constant and perpetual state of denial. I was able to continue my life because, even after leaving college and spending four years in the military, his mother and I rarely communicated. The only news I received about my son was through family members, even when returning home from leave of duty, once in a while. By being away from home for so many years, my thought of him not being my son was supported by my denial and removal from this apparent reality. For the most part, I lived in denial and conducted my life as if my son was not mine. Being in denial is how I mentally managed to be separated from my son without feeling completely guilty.

Several years passed without seeing or getting to know my son. When I was discharged from the military in 1975, I didn't return home but made residence in New York City. Suffice to say, I didn't return to St. Louis very often. However, when I did on several occasions, mostly during holidays, my mother would invite my son to our home so that I would see him while I was in town. I am not proud of the fact that it was strictly my mother's doing for me to see and talk to my son. Sadly to say, if she had not done so, it would have been fine with me. However, when I saw him, we would casually talk, not ever broaching the subject why his mom and I never communicated regularly or why I didn't play a major role in his life. He was about twelve or thirteen. When we talked, I would simply advise him to stay in school and give him a little spending money. Unfortunately, there were only brief encounters with my son before his life was abruptly shortened at the tender age of twenty-seven. He was in his late teens by the time my wife and three daughters met him for the first time. I had mentioned him to my wife when he was much younger, but I had never told my daughters they potentially had an older brother. When my daughters met my son, they liked him and immediately welcomed him into our family, even after my maintaining it was a possibility he may not be my son. I continued to have mixed emotions about him being my son because I had never gotten a DNA test to confirm whether or not he was, in fact, my son. I equivocated about the reality of having a son for many years, although deep within my soul I believed he was my son. Quite frankly, I did not want to know the truth.

By not admitting definitively to my wife that he was my son, it caused a rift between my mother and my wife, which was difficult for me to manage. When we visited St. Louis, my mom would consistently talk about my son in definitive terms, trying to encourage me to play more of a role in his life. My wife, on the other hand, reacted negatively about my mom's insistence, and rightly so, because I consistently led her to believe that I had serious doubts about whether or not he was actually my son. My wife believed my mother was adding another child to our family because I led her to believe there still remained such questionable doubt. The thought of having tension between my wife and mother was daunting and problematic because they were the two most influential women in my life. I didn't handle the situation very well, and the problem festered longer than I would have liked.

A reality check and turning point in this whole saga began when my mother showed me a picture of my son and his mother. At first glance, I thought it was me in the photo but knew instinctively it could not have been because his mother was three years younger than I. In the photo, his mother appeared to be in her early thirties, and he seemed about eighteen. My son looked exactly like me when I was his age. It was at that moment and from that point on that I fully accepted him as my son. By this time, my son was in his early twenties when I truly considered him part of my flesh and blood. I did not realize and never understood how rough it was for my son growing up until family members shared with me his troubled childhood, which over time negatively affected his mental state of mind. He had other younger sisters and brothers whom he grew up with, and to my knowledge, he was raised without the solid support and guidance from their mother or father. I never met his other siblings.

Later I discovered, through my older sister, the extent of my son's mental condition. He had developed mental problems in his late teens and was taking medication to control some inherent anxieties of which I was unaware. My son and I eventually had a heart-to- heart talk. I told him how sorry I was for not being a father to him and asked for his forgiveness. He told me he always loved me and that never changed. He also said he was never resentful of the fact that I was not present in his life while growing up, but he missed my being part of his life as a father. Both of us felt the painful and brutal reality of not having had a natural father-son relationship. At that moment, neither of us could hold back tears. We had missed so much of each other's lives being apart. Considering the many years of neglect and absence in my son's life, I sensed no bitterness or resentment toward me, which is a testament to his forgiving spirit and undeniable strength of character. Although, at the time, he and his mother lived in St. Louis while I lived in West Virginia, my son and I became closer than I could have ever imagined, but it seemed a little too late. We did not see each other very often, but we talked. By this time, I began to feel guilty because I had not been a primary influence in his life while he was growing up, but the guilt I felt was nothing like what was to come. I thought, if only I had taken the time to know him and spend time with him, his life would have been different and more stable. He was then in his early twenties, mentally unstable, and not sure about his future. I actually considered moving him to West Virginia to live with us, but after carefully considering his age and mental state, I decided it would not be prudent to move him into our home. Occasionally we would talk over the phone, but there was one particular time while talking that I realized how troubled he was because he stated he considered taking his own life. He sounded very depressed and confused, as if he were unsure of where his life was going. I really didn't know what to say at that moment but to assure him things would get better, and I pleaded with him not to ever think that way.

## Final Annals of Guilt

I have just shared the backdrop of the relationship between my son and me, at least what little we had. Now I need to explain how things ended in this regard. It was in the mid-1990s on a late night in June when a family member informed me that my son had died. I was told he was found along the banks of the Des Peres River and had been dead for nearly two weeks before someone discovered his body. This was news I didn't want to hear but was forced to accept. I was stunned, shocked, and petrified at the thought he was no longer living. After hearing this shocking and dreadful news, I seemed to have entered an emotional cesspool, and the real guilt hit me like a ton of bricks. Just when I was beginning to know and have a sagacious relationship with my son, the last thing I would have expected happened. Over and over in my mind, I could not remove the thought of my first and only son being dead and gone. All I could think about was the fact I had not been part of his life during all those years when he needed me, his father. Even until his death, I was not there to guide and protect him from danger. Tears began to fall down my cheeks incessantly.

I've done many things in life I'm not proud of, but nothing has ever elicited the emotions and crushing guilt I experienced for the next several months. To attend his funeral, I drove eight hours to St. Louis in desperate tears, trying to overcome the guilt I felt for not being a father to my son. When I went to his funeral, his casket was closed and sealed from viewing because of the decomposition his body had endured before being found. The fact that I could not see my son for the very last time was even more painful and emotionally oppressive. I continued to feel the intense guilt during the eight- hour drive back to West Virginia, and I could not fight back the agonizing tears that seemed to have dismantled my balance of peace. This was just the beginning because the guilt I felt was grievous and unbearable.

For several months, the guilt was so profound it was difficult to properly carry out normal daily functions without thinking things could have been different with my son if only I had lived up to my responsibility of being a father to him. The guilt I carried was perpetual and obviously began to affect my mental acuity. It was like carrying a heavy load on my shoulders. My peace of mind was certainly jeopardized by this seemingly intensified strange emotion, which I had never confronted. I knew I needed deliverance but had kept hidden this past misguided behavior. I did not want anyone to know how irresponsible I had been, but the shame and guilt were overwhelming.

Finally, during a small group meeting with church members, I was compelled to tell my burdensome truth that had plagued me for months. After telling these devout members of the church my story, they fell to their knees and prayed for me. The impact of their prayers was so confirming it led me to uncontrollable tears, and the burden of my guilt was lifted immediately. I thank God for those sincere prayers that reinforced how impactful prayers can be, forever believing that prayers change things. There is nothing like a praying group of spiritual-minded folk like those who interceded for me. I still occasionally think of my son's demise and how I miss him, but I never look back to the shame and guilt I carried because of that particular past profound neglect. I thank God I regained my peace. My late son's name is Delancey L. Ray. RIP.

# CHAPTER 11

## The Deep Pit of My Pieces

I GREW UP AROUND PEOPLE WHO DRANK alcohol like it was a common beverage. I remember many family gatherings during holidays and other occasions where drinking was normal. These included my father, uncle, aunts, and one or two older cousins, some of whom may have been alcoholics, but if so, I was unaware. Therefore, when I became of age to drink, I didn't bat an eye. I started drinking just before I left high school, but after graduating, I began to drink more and more and dabbled with almost every drink you could name, from rum, bourbon, whisky, vodka, gin, to wine and even cough medicine. I drank excessively, got drunk on several occasions, and passed out because I couldn't hold liquor very well. My siblings can certainly attest to this because they have old pictures and tease me periodically about my past behavior.

This pattern continued for about one year, but the drinking was a precursor to later experimentation with other drugs, such as barbiturates and amphetamines, including consumption of marijuana. Although my experiential drinking and drug consumption was short- lived, the fact that I engaged in this conduct was indicative of my willingness to go beyond certain boundaries I had been taught not to. By the time I joined the navy, I had stopped the heavy drinking and doing drugs. Although the guilt from my neglect regarding my son had desisted, I was faced with a more insidious challenge in my life. As I believe, a residual and hidden psychological scar began to manifest shortly after his death. I, without considering the consequences, began to, as I had in the past, occasionally do drugs, which spiraled into a regrettable addiction. This, in my view, was the beginning of what I believe to be the lowest point in my life, the pit of my life's journey. This particular adventure began intermittingly while in my late forties and came to a head while in my fifties. My wildest imagination would have never conceived of this unfortunate and despicable behavior. I believe the seed of my inclination to experiment with alcohol and drugs had been supplanted many years before I started drinking. My proclivity to drink or do drugs had been dormant for many years before I began to try drugs again, and unfortunately, when I did, of all drugs, I chose cocaine. My knowledge of cocaine and its effects was limited, although I was not totally ignorant of the behavior and consequences of those who indulged in it. I actually believed it could never happen to me, but I took the bait and began to smoke, in its rock form, crack cocaine. This was one of the biggest mistakes of my life, and I paid a huge price for it. When I began to smoke the cocaine substance, it was sporadic at first but eventually took me into a nightmare of despair and desperation for deliverance. I never envisioned this drug would have the power it had over me because I had never driven myself so low into deception and unsound thinking. Over a short period of time, I found myself undoubtedly hooked on crack.

    This part of my journey began in St. Louis, my hometown, where I took my first hit on a crack pipe only hours away from Charleston, West Virginia, where I lived. St. Louis was an eight-hour drive from Charleston, and I would visit there frequently because of the short distance. It was the first time I had lived so close to the town where I grew up. My commencement with drugs began while visiting my hometown for a family gathering at a familiar park. A small group of about five left the park to purchase alcohol but instead made a quick stop at a close relative's home to smoke some herbs. To my surprise, someone introduced us to the rock or "crack," and for some moronic reason, I saw no harm in trying it for the first time. While smoking, I felt no pain and believed it was just an innocent experiment. I left St. Louis thinking I had violated a fundamental belief of abstaining from any substance of this kind but quickly dismissed my one-time indulgence. What I didn't see coming was my inclination to try it again, and again, and again. I had temporarily forgotten a basic rule of behavior: if you don't try it, you won't miss it. I had not considered my propensity or willingness to try new things, which included past binges with alcohol and less addictive drugs.

Thereafter, I would frequently visit St. Louis for a couple days, and when I did, I would smoke crack, which became a pattern over a few years. When I would smoke this stuff, the rush I felt from just one hit was so gratifying I would crave more and more to the point I didn't want to leave to return home. The sensation of one puff made me realize why those who become addicted behave in the destructive way they do. However, strangely enough, I did not smoke it when I returned to Charleston, and there would sometimes be months between my visits to St. Louis where I actually began this awful trip to insanity. My being able to function normally, of course, gave me a false sense of security, in that I thought I was different and could never become addicted to this particular drug, which has, in reality, killed and ruined so many lives. After a couple years of this behavior, I firmly believed and convinced myself it would never happen to me.

## Roadbed to Addiction

My worst nightmare was realized after moving to Maryland and being confronted with an opportunity to buy and indulge consistently with this elicit product on a regular basis. Prior to being captivated by this drug, I was gaining weight and reached nearly two hundred pounds. My average weight had been typically around 185 pounds, so I joined a fitness center near my job and worked out at least twice a week. After a month or two, I began to lose a little weight but not much. But my weight loss became more evident and was eventually compounded from the lack of appetite when the drugs replaced daily food and nutrients. As with many things, it was a gradual process where, in the beginning, I began using crack only once a month, and over time, once a week and eventually three to five days in one week. Within a year, my weight fell from two hundred pounds to 145 pounds. At first, I was completely fine with the weight loss because my clothes seemed to fit better, and ironically my blood pressure stats had improved. I had not yet realized the deprivation of food was destroying and compromising my physical health. But I steadfastly continued this destructive behavior for several years. To others, especially my wife, my weight loss became an issue and appeared to be a sign that something was wrong. My wife would constantly ask me if I was all right and eventually began to worry that my health was failing. At this point, she was uncertain and thought I just didn't want to talk about it. However, I played it off as best I could and claimed the weight loss was due to physical training, which was true initially. In reality, I actually began to look ill and malnourished. Overall, I had loss a tremendous amount of weight, and my sunken facial structure, in particular, made me literally look sick, and by then I was, in fact, both mentally and physically ill.

Of course, I kept up the pretense that nothing was wrong, and I especially didn't want to face the fact that I needed help. Although my wife had no idea of my habitual drug use, she grew more and more concerned about my health. There was certainly no way of her knowing the extent of my addiction because the only sign of something wrong was my physical appearance. I continued to pay the bills, and our finances were still intact from my and her earnings. The money I used for the drugs was in a separate account from my credit union, or I should say, an account we had accumulated several thousand dollars of which I was personally able to draw from without her knowledge.

# Heading toward the Abyss

In the midst of my drug addiction, a lack of my mental acuity became so protracted I began to accuse my wife of having an affair. She would insist she had not and was completely stunned by my accusations. It was then that she really began to become most concerned of my physical health and questioned my behavior because they both appeared to be dissimilar from my normal physical and mental disposition. To be honest, I had no evidence to suggest my wife was having an affair, but in my mind, I somehow rationalized otherwise. Things went quickly downhill because we seemed to argue daily, and our relationship began to erode like never before. This was certainly a wake-up call for me, but I refused to stop. I was in too deep to quit. But with what little honestly I had left in me, I decided to tell her the truth about my drug indulgence, and it wasn't easy. Although I confessed to my drug use, I did not confess and refused to admit to the power and control the drugs had over me. When I told her I was using cocaine, in the form of crack, she was terribly disturbed and rightly so. My confession to her concerning my drug use created a void between us and caused a tenser environment for communication. At this point, it seemed we were unable to communicate freely because of her aversion to my drug use and my unwillingness to admit the obvious—I was addicted to crack.

I quickly came to the notion that I must tell my daughters about my drug use, and it wasn't easy. After informing them, I felt humiliated with disgrace, and I was subjugated to shame. They had always regarded me as a devout Christian, good husband to their mother, and exceptional father and provider for them. Even though they showed some compassion for my predicament, I knew it was a great disappointment, as it was to my wife. I was undoubtedly concerned they had lost respect for me, but I remained in my crisis, convinced I was functional and the drug use was just a passing experiment. After a so-called family intervention, my wife and I decided to see a therapist to get a handle on our disintegrating relationship. The counseling only lasted for about a month or two before I decided to stop attending the sessions because I felt I was being double-teamed by my wife and the female counselor. It was truly an irrational act, but my drug addiction was in control of my thoughts and behavior.

As I continued into a downward spin, my addiction got worse and led to unbelievable dimensions. By this time, I had become accustomed to the drug culture. I had no idea or foresight of how entrenched I would become within this illegal and illicit drug culture. I found myself deep within the traditional quagmire of drugs and deception. I knew many dealers from whom I could purchase the drugs and met many drug users who indulged with the same intensity and fulfillment as I. The abuse from the drugs to both my mind and body had reached such critical proportions that my sense of self had become obtuse and reduced to not getting the proper sleep, not eating nutritionally, and having a lack of basic hygiene. I had not accepted the fact that this drug was not only affecting my mental capacity to think clearly but also, to a greater extent, my physical health. I was immobilized to the extent I became depressed and consciously paranoid. The paranoia became normal and commonplace for me. Every time I left my home I would believe I was being followed. I believed I was being followed by the law enforcement, by the Federal Bureau of Investigations (FBI), and by drug dealers to see what I was up to. I even believed my wife had hired an investigator to track my whereabouts. Due to my paranoia, I created all types of diversionary tactics while driving to avoid being followed — occasionally pulling over to the side of the road, making quick and unnecessary U-turns, and monitoring license plates. Ironically, in my continued use of this hideous and destructive drug, I seemed to be in a comfortable place, not realizing I was in the abyss of my addiction. I was sick and didn't know it. The effects of my addiction began to spread across familiar boundaries. My wife had become so mortified and angry that she wanted space between us and considered moving from our home. Other family members became aware of my addiction and were obviously concerned about my physical and mental health.

As the savings we had accrued in my credit union account were being depleted, I began to create more debts by opening new credit cards, which began to harm our overall financial stability. My ability to think clearly was certainly being affected. The drugs were affecting my ability to perform routine tasks at work. As I approached my rock bottom, the seriousness of my condition was overwhelming. Our financial stability was being seriously compromised. I was on the verge of losing my wife, my job, my home, and everything we had worked together to accomplish. At this point, I began to consider rehabilitative treatment. But prior to that, my wife appeared to be very combative with me and I could do no right. I felt, at the time, she literally hated me to her core for what I was putting her through, and I felt she had turned her back on me while I was at the lowest point in my life. I felt I had no refuge and she could not possibly understand what I was going through. What I wanted was an enabler, which she was not. In her defense, she had no clue of how to deal with my problem, which became hers by default, especially considering it was someone as close as I, her husband. It had a profound effect on her, and I could not begin to conceive its impact to her consciousness. She did the best she could, under the circumstances, to help and understand my addiction.

On several occasions, she pleaded with me to get help, and she attended NA meetings for those with drug-addicted family members. She also reached out to the clergy for help and spoke to several of my immediate family for support. My sister who is one year younger gave considerable attention to my health and well-being. As I would accuse my wife of different things, my sister would always interject that it was the drugs causing the discord and that it would pass once I got help. She, at that time, seemed to be the only one I could talk to, the bridge to my true sanity. She became my confidante and played a significant role toward the recovery of my addiction. These and other factors helped me to finally muster enough mental awareness to at least acknowledge I needed help and to recognize I didn't have the strength or power to turn my life around and to certainly admit I was not able to do it alone. Prior to treatment, I was embarrassed, ashamed, clouded by guilt, and totally despondent. I knew it was time for me to get help I desperately needed. My wife's attitude and total disgust with my predicament, I must say, played a huge role in my final decision to seek help.

## Call to Action

Eventually, my wife found a treatment center located in south Florida, several hundred miles from where we lived in Maryland. The treatment center made all the arrangements for my stay and purchased a one-way ticket to Florida, knowing it would take weeks for my initial recovery. This meant I had to take off from work for an extended period. Due to the embarrassing nature of my problem, I told my boss an elaborate story to justify my absence. I had adequate leave; therefore, it was a minor issue. Things were all set in place for me to leave for rehabilitation. I was serious about my potential recovery. However, the day before I was slated to leave, I bought three rocks of crack cocaine valued at fifty dollars per rock. I figured I would indulge for the last time and splurge the night before I left, having in mind to never pick up a crack pipe again. I was up all night smoking this stuff and thought it would be over by early morning before leaving home, but by morning, I had one remaining rock. Now it was time to leave, but instead of disposing of the rock, I hid it in a place where no one but me could find it. In the back of my mind, I knew it was a mistake, but my disease had matured to a point where I could not think clearly. As we left for the airport, my wife drove. I could not remove the thought and fact I had stashed and left a rock of cocaine back home. In my mind, I knew I would probably not have the strength to discard the rock when I returned home from rehabilitation, but in reality, I simply wanted to smoke the rest of it. The idea continued to trouble me even after reaching the airport to board my flight. More and more, I thought about the idea of smoking the rock I left behind. Just before boarding, I had resigned in my mind I could not take this trip with that huge rock left behind, and I decided to not take the flight. My wife had no idea of my troubling thoughts and was pleased that I was on the way to begin the recovery from this deadly disease of which I had become captive. Just prior to boarding, I mentioned to my wife I did not feel well and could not take the flight. She was very angry and frustrated with my insistence not to board the plane and suggested I call the treatment center to convince me otherwise. I called the treatment center to tell them what I had told my wife, and they knew right away it was the drugs talking and tried to convince me to change my mind, but I was determined to get back to that rock I had left behind, and no one could convince me otherwise.

Obviously, I did not take the flight, which caused a huge dispute between my wife and me because she did not want to take me back to the house. This would have been no problem for me, but I didn't have a dime to my name, and there was no other way I could get home without my wife taking me there. She finally gave in, but when we reached the house, another big argument ensued. She had no idea that all I wanted was to get my hands on the crack I had left behind. Without much other discussion, I got my rock and decided to stay at a nearby hotel to freely support my habit, and I left. I used a credit card to check into a nearby hotel and smoked the remains of what I had left behind. When it was all done, I called the treatment center back and told them I was ready to come. They arranged for another flight late that evening, and I was then on my way to being treated for my disease.

# Steps toward Recovery

When I arrived at the treatment center late that night, I was welcomed with open arms. The check-in process was very thorough, and I immediately thought to myself this was a real start to recovery and that this nightmare would be over soon, but in retrospect, it was only the beginning. The next day, I realized that this facility was a holding post for detox treatment because many patients who entered had multiple addictions, some of which required treatment for physical withdrawal symptoms. During and before my addiction to cocaine, my alcohol consumption was almost nonexistent and limited to a few beers or few glasses of wine on a social basis, but my treatment was for both. What I did not realize was that my treatment for alcohol would be just as intense as it would be for the cocaine use. However, that was okay with me because it didn't matter. I was simply fortunate to receive help for a problem that negatively impacted me and my family. The treatment center held hundreds of incoming patients for an initial detox treatment. I met people of all stripes and colors, educated and uneducated, poor and some with wealth. Addictions have no preference. I was under the misguided assumption that most addicts were there to be treated for alcohol and illegal drug abuse but stunned to discover that the majority were there to be treated because of prescription drug dependency. These addictions included drugs like Vicodin, Oxycodone, Percocet, Opiate, and many others. I didn't realize addictions from these drugs were such an epidemic across our country until I entered this treatment center. The detox treatment varied from patient to patient but for me about three days before being transferred to another location where I would stay for the rest of my treatment. This housing complex accommodated nearly a hundred recovering addicts. It was the beginning of many sessions that were essential to understanding my addiction and how to deal with underlying mental or behavior health issues. The food was great and nourishing, a refreshing change from my old eating habits. However, most importantly, the treatment for my addiction was comprehensive with one-on-one therapy, group therapy, twelve-step meetings, and other individualized treatment groups. I met many with all kinds of addictions and became comfortable with the fact that we were all in the same boat and had very interesting stories to tell about what led us to the treatment center.

The treatment center paved a way for me to get well again and return to a normal life. The things I learned about substance abuse and the tools they provided to avoid the same old lifestyle I developed in my addiction were invaluable. At the end of about five weeks of treatment, I was confident and ready to return to normalcy with my family and friends. I had met many addicts who had returned to the center for a second time, but I knew and vowed I would never be one of those who left and relapsed. I recall the first day of my treatment I was told by a firm alcoholic that this was his second time around. He told me he relapsed a day or two after leaving the treatment center the first time. He apparently hooked up with people in his past who consumed alcohol; he had one drink, and before he knew it, he was back to where he had been before his first treatment. Obviously, he had ignored one of the first principles of being sober, which was to stay away from the previous environments conducive to repeating old habits, to avoid people who indulged in your weakness that led to your predicament, and to not repeat the same old habits that would lead to the same outcomes. Essentially, they are people, places, and things that are three commitments any addict must make and put into practice to fully recover.

Upon leaving the treatment center, I vowed to never again return to drugs or place myself in an environment that would potentially feed my old habits. When I returned home, I was confident of my recovery, but I felt I still needed support in my desire to stay sober, so I attended an outpatient clinic a couple times a week. I was determined not to relapse, unlike many of those I had met at the rehab center who returned for treatment two and three times after formally being rehabilitated. As I began my journey in recovery, I was constantly reminded I was no different from anyone else, but if I were truly committed to staying sober, I certainly could, and I did for a while. About nine months into my recovery, the very thing I had witnessed through others and dreaded happened. I relapsed because I became complacent and began to place myself in the same past familiar environments that led to my addiction. I began to smoke again and initially cringed at the idea I was back into an old habit that impeded my ability to function in a sane and productive manner. Within a blink, I had succumbed to the thought of pleasure and desire to get high again even as I continued to attend the outpatient addiction treatment center. Although the clinic employed random checks for sobriety through taking urine samples, I continued to consume the drugs to support my addiction, which had once seemed to have been well managed. Over time, my indulgence of the drug caught up with me when my urine samples came up positive. At this point, the treatment center advised that I return to an inpatient center for a second time, but I was not prepared to do so, and I stopped attending the clinic. I again was captured in the malaise of my disease and certainly didn't want to admit I was that bad off, enough to require returning to rehab treatment center.

What complicated my thoughts was that things had gotten much better at home, and I had begun to enjoy a peaceful and normal life again. The last thing I wanted to do was to admit to my wife I had begun to use again. Because my use of the drugs was much less than before, I believed I could manage it and gradually quit. However, it didn't work that way. As I continued to use, I began to smoke more, and I began to manifest a behavior similar to what it was like before my first rehabilitation effort. As a result, my wife became suspicious and voiced her concerns that I might be doing drugs again. As much as I tried to deny the fact I was using again, it became more evident through my behavior that I was, and I could not hide it anymore. I tried to convince my wife that this was a slight setback but was manageable and I would stop. To demonstrate my sincerity of quitting, and I was sincere, we decided to purchase over-the-counter drug kits to show if I was still doing drugs.

Over time, I tried very hard to stop, but I was still drawn to my original addiction and on occasion would come up positive for drug use. Again, I simply could not quit on my own. No matter how much my wife wanted to believe I had the will and strength to quit, she was very frustrated and disgusted with the idea that I had returned to drugs again. Our relationship was, once again, muted with conflict, pain, and dissention because I could not accept the obvious.

My wife and I had been married many years, and this predicament was the one thing to end a long, enduring relationship. I needed help and could not do it alone. This dilemma for my wife and me lasted a few months before I decided to seek help again. This time I sought a therapist who I thought could help me understand the basis for my addiction and uncover any underlying mental issues that sustained my substance abuse. I also believed seeking this type of counsel would help foil further unknown underlying rifts between my wife and me that may have existed prior to my addiction. The therapeutic sessions were meaningful and allowed me to talk my way through troubling aspects of my childhood's development. They helped to put certain things in perspective, but they were not enough to terminate my primordial desire to continue using the drugs.

At some point, I began to question my faith in God, but just as I did, I heard a voice say, "I called you when you were a young boy, and you are mine." The voice was not audible but was clear in my mind, just as if someone in the same room had spoken to me. The thought took me all the way back to my childhood when I was first exposed to his love and forgiveness. From that day forward, I took this to mean I was, in fact, a child of God's, and I refused to believe anyone who would judge me differently. I believe he allowed me to succumb to this state of despair to show me his abundant love and saving grace.

Because I was still in my addictive state, I knew I had to make a move. In my mind, I had two reasonable options—return to an inpatient center for rehabilitation or attend another outpatient clinic to assist in my recovery. I decided to do the latter and began attending another outpatient clinic. This was another big step for me but was not met with much excitement because I truly did not want to do this again. Even in this diseased state of mind, I reasoned I could get my sanity back. I also surmised it would not only help toward my recovery from this dreadful sickness but also help to repair and salvage my marriage. I didn't realize it at the time, but my initial visit to the clinic was the best decision I could have made because it proved to have paved a realistic path to my eventual recovery.

My first meeting was with a fairly large group of other drug users, about thirty or so, some who attended voluntarily as myself and some involuntarily because of a court order. Nevertheless, the goals were the same, to overcome the drug use and discontinue past destructive behaviors. As we gathered and waited for the individual who would be conducting the session, I thought to myself and asked, *How did I get here and how will I get out of this predicament?* As I pondered more, a very tall, personable man walked into the room and began to welcome the group. As he began to speak and while sharing his life history of drugs and recovery, deep within my soul, I knew he would be the one who would assist in my recovery. His story was compelling, and my addiction was nothing compared to what he had gone through. I felt strongly that he was sent by God to personally help me overcome my addiction, and I sincerely believe I was right. After the session was over, I quickly approached him and asked if he could help me one-on-one to rid myself of my addiction, outside of the clinic's environment, and he said yes he would. I was delighted because I believed this was a true sign of my being healed of this dreadful disease. We met on a weekly basis for several months, and gradually my pain, my shame, my guilt, and my desire to use was diminished to a point where I became normal again and began to function as I did prior to my addiction. I must be honest and admit it was not an easy road to travel. During this process, the most challenging thing for me was to get rid of my cell phone, as he advised me to do in the very beginning of our sessions, but I stubbornly refused. He knew and recognized the one thing getting in the way of my final recovery was having a cell phone where I had developed so many contacts with the drug community. I reluctantly but finally took his advice, and shortly after, I was well on the way to recovery. Without his help, I wonder how far along the recovery spectrum I would be. In the end, it was worthwhile, and I thank God because I am drug- free. He also worked at a county corrections facility where he helped inmates work through the criminal justice system and supported them toward their exit into society at large again. After my recovery, about every three months or so, he would ask me to speak to the inmates (men and women), to tell my story, which I was more than happy to do. A few years ago, my friend and confidant passed in his sleep. His name is Greg Wright. RIP.

## Close Encounters with Darkness

Throughout the course of my experience with this drug and from the early trappings of my addiction, I encountered many sobering moments, signs, or red flags to signal real danger. The dispassionate moments were obvious indications when I passed out on several occasions. By my count, I fainted seven times during my obsession with the drug, but I could not find the will to stop. My first wake-up call began early into my addiction. I was at a supermarket while attempting to get money from an ATM. All of a sudden, I felt faint, and the next thing I knew I was on the floor regaining consciousness while several onlookers watched, wondering what had happened. When I fell, my head and neck hit the hard ground, with such tremendous force I had to be rushed to the hospital, where I remained for one week, suffering excruciating pain, especially over the first few days. The diagnosis from the impact of my fall resulted in a pinched nerve on the lower vertebra of my neck, which brought about symptoms of numbness and needle-like sensations on the tips of my fingers. I endured thirteen weeks of therapy before the symptoms completely diminished.

I passed out on several other occasions, all taking place in four different states. Each time I was rushed to the hospital not knowing what the outcome would be. The last time my life was seriously compromised while doing drugs was when I lost consciousness on a busy interstate. I left Maryland the evening before Thanksgiving, heading toward St. Louis to spend time with family for Thanksgiving. It was about seven or eight at night, four hours outside of St. Louis, when I began to feel faint while smoking crack and driving on Interstate 64. I knew exactly what to expect next. I would pass out; I had experienced this feeling several times before. Knowing this, I slowed down, hit the hazard lights, and quickly pulled off the road, I thought, before passing out. When I regained consciousness, to my dismay, I realized I had not fully pulled over to the roadside but had stopped in the right-hand lane of the interstate. I quickly pulled to the side to regain my strength before continuing my trip to St. Louis. At that moment, a police officer pulled behind me, got out of his car, approached me, and asked questions I could not answer. I immediately interjected that I had passed out and just regained consciousness. He then asked if I was on the interstate when I stopped, and I affirmed that I was. Apparently there had been several calls to 911 that a vehicle was parked on the right lane of the interstate. I don't know how long I was unconscious, but it was without a doubt my car standing on the interstate. After requesting my driver's license and registration, he returned to his car to check the validity of my registration and plate information.

Afterwards, he left without further incident. I was lucky he didn't search my car because if he had, he would have found the remaining drugs and paraphernalia in the car. I could have been arrested and faced with a criminal charge. After sitting for another moment or two, I began to drive again, hoping I'd reach St. Louis soon, but I still felt very weak. At this point, I thought the most prudent thing to do was to find a hotel for the night and continue the next day. As I traveled further down the interstate, I found a motel where I could rest, thinking I could then resume my trip early the next morning. Approximately a mile down the road was a small establishment where mostly truckers stop to rest and eat. Still very weak, I managed to make it to the front desk, but while checking in, I felt faint again. The next thing I realized was that I regaining consciousness again but this time on the floor in front of where customers check in and out of the motel. By this time, paramedics had arrived and were prepared to rush me to the hospital after checking my vital signs. My initial inclination, when I regained consciousness, was to refuse to be taken to the hospital, but as I raised my head, I felt faint again and decided to submit. Because of guilt and shame, I didn't want my family to know what happened. Guilt, because I allowed myself to be in this predicament, and shame from the stigma associated with my drug problem. This was the night before Thanksgiving, and everyone expected me to arrive in St. Louis sometime that night. Of course, I had to let someone know what happened. I believe I called my wife, and of course everyone found out I was laid up in a county hospital somewhere in Kentucky. I was released from the hospital Thanksgiving day. My father, brother, and brother-in-law drove to Kentucky to drive me and my car back to St. Louis. I was grateful they did, but my pride muted and masked a good part of my consciousness.

One other very serious implication of my addiction was being stopped and approached by a police officer while smoking crack. This was one more incident added to my un-fortuitous moments of being accosted by an officer of the law. It appeared I was always on a mission to get high, not recognizing the gravity of my actions. One cool and chilly late afternoon, I was on my way to meet someone, but before reaching them, and to satisfy my primal desire, I stopped on the side of the road and got out of my car to smoke. While doing so, a police officer drove up beside me and asked what was I doing. Of course, I immediately responded that I was smoking a cigarette, but the officer knew better because she had watched me from a distance without my knowledge. Stunned by this unforeseen encroachment to my sensibilities, I dropped my crack pipe on the ground, hoping she did not notice, but she did. Every fiber within my clustered imagination was dismantled because I knew I was in big trouble. I was faced with the prospect of being carted to jail and convicted of using an illegal substance. I immediately took a blameworthy posture and began to explain my addictive behavior. Ironically, I had met with my wife and daughters a few weeks prior about my addiction and promised to stop smoking. I conveyed this to the officer and conceded my error and lack of sound judgment. I explained I was in the process of getting help, and I humbly pleaded for mercy. After about a half hour of talking, to my delight, the officer graciously gave me her card and allowed me to go on my way.

## Unintended Consequences

There were two other occasions that were a little more pernicious or problematic because I was in recovery from my drug use. It was a summer's hot day during a Sunday morning service when I felt faint and began to sweat profusely. My body became weak and almost limp as a wet noodle. At this point, my wife realized something was wrong and immediately asked for help. I was quickly taken outside in a wheelchair for fresh air, but still there was no sign of comfort. Someone called 911 for help, and paramedics arrived on the scene within minutes. After observing my vital signs, they whisked me off to the hospital. I was in the hospital for more than five hours before a doctor came to me and said I needed a stent and an angioplasty had to be performed. I took the doctor's word and allowed him to perform the operation, which was not very long, but I remained in the hospital a few days.

After I was discharged from the hospital, I called my personal cardiologist for a follow-up. Now here's the troubling part of the matter. After he examined me and viewed my hospital records from the procedure, he admitted to me, in unequivocal terms, a stent was not needed, and the surgery was unnecessary. His disclosure was very disconcerting because the stent could not be removed and would remain with me for the rest of my life. The operation was a mental setback because I was put on several prescription drugs for nearly six months to supposedly keep me in good health.

Another troubling incident occurred when I was on a plane headed to St. Louis for a family reunion. I had rushed to get to the airport during early morning rush hour, and I thought I would be late, but I made the flight on time. Thinking I would be late, I had built up quite a bit of anxiety and did not feel comfortable. I was sitting in a window seat, and before the plane approached the runway, the pilot indicated there would be a delay, so the plane sat on the tarmac's runway for a while. While waiting, I began to feel faint, just as I did on previous occasions. The next thing I knew, I was regaining consciousness, and a paramedic was on board asking me questions I could not answer because I was too weak to respond. I was taken off the plane on a stretcher and rushed to the hospital. On the way to the hospital, the attending paramedic of thirty years took my vital signs and was convinced I had a heart attack. When I arrived at the hospital, doctors surrounded my bed to diagnose the cause of my blackout but determined I did not have a heart attack. They asserted my blood pressure dropped too low, causing me to faint, and they surmised I was probably dehydrated. Suffice to say, I missed the flight and the family reunion. Again, I was not doing drugs when these two incidents occurred. They happened later during my recovery but may have been residual effects from my drug use.

After this entire ordeal, I asked myself, why was I protected on the interstate without being harmed? Why was I stopped by an officer of the law twice without being charged for using an illegal substance? How did I faint several times without passing from this life? It can only be explained through divine intervention. There is no doubt that the grace of God was covering me and my path during all of these, what should have been, sobering moments. It seems ironic but makes a lot of sense; that is, God allowed me to wallow in this particular cesspool but was always with me. My wife and I remain together and recently celebrated our fortieth anniversary. I retired from my job at age fifty-six after thirty-two years, our financial state is stable, and we are able to enjoy the latter years of our lives.

It is a testament to God's unconditional love that brought me out of that mess. I am thankful to him and, with a sound mind, able to share this particular part of my life's journey. As I walked this path of misery, I now realize how it impacted my wife and would like to share her original thoughts and perspective of what she had to endure during this torrential time in our lives. The following chapter captures her true feelings and emotional ride through the deep part of my life's struggles.

# CHAPTER 12

## Deep Pit of Pieces—Part II
## (My Wife's Perspective)

We had moved to Maryland from West Virginia about four years earlier and had just bought our dream house and what I hoped would be our last home. Michael and I had somewhat drifted apart, meaning we had stopped having real meaningful conversations. We talked, but our talks were mainly about the children, an incident here and there, much like many married couples who were married for more than twenty years. We were comfortable and didn't put out much effort with each other. I think usually when the interest in the marriage is in this stage, couples find mini distractions and make those their focus instead of focusing on repairing their strained relationship.

The year before all hell broke loose in our house, we had houseguests staying with us. One of Michael's West Virginia friend's wife came to stay with us. This was not the original intent. The friend was supposed to come and stay for a few months to seek employment in Maryland. While he was here, he was supposed to find housing and prepare for his family's arrival. Somehow, I'm not sure how, things changed. His wife and teenage sons came instead. The job never materialized. The husband never came. The wife and two teenage boys stayed in our home for the entire school year. Our three girls who had just graduated from college had also moved back home. This houseguest drama is a story in itself, but I won't take the time to tell it now.

Right after all the drama of getting this family out of our home ended, Michael and I, with no other momentary distractions, began paying attention to each other, or at least I began to pay attention to him. There's nothing like an outside enemy to force a couple to cling together. Shortly after the wife and teenage sons moved, I began to notice that Michael had lost a lot of weight. I had noticed before now that his legs were getting smaller but didn't make much of it. Now I began to realize not only were his legs getting smaller, his body was smaller. He was losing weight, and it was noticeable because his clothes no longer fit. I honestly thought he had a deadly disease and braced myself to hear he was dying, and maybe me too. He was spending a great deal of time locked up in the bathroom, but he had always been a bit secretive that way. When we first got married, I thought he was having an affair because he would disappear for short periods and wouldn't say where he had been. He would also take phone calls in private, and my new wife's mind immediately went the affair route. I later found out he was a secret smoker, ashamed of this addiction he had hidden from me and the girls.

Anyway, after becoming alarmed that my husband was dying, I decided we needed to talk. I remember both of us in the bedroom, and me telling him something to the effect that whatever it was, he could tell me. I had watched a lot of *Oprah* and other relationship shows and had read a great deal of relationship books and looked at numerous video presentations on relationships. Michael, being Michael, saw this as an opportunity to unburden and tell the truth. I don't think Michael was ever the type of person to perpetuate a lie and enjoy the deception. So he began to confess. To this day, all I remember was him saying drugs and crack and that he could quit any time and would quit now.

Like Michael, I was a churchgoer. When my siblings and I were very young, my mother sent us to an Episcopal church about a block from our house, for Sunday school every Sunday. When I was about eleven years old, my father took us out of that church and introduced us to the Pentecostal church, where I would spend the bulk of my adult churchgoing. I spent my life living inside the boundaries that the church and I had set for me. My fear of going to hell made me live very carefully. I bought into the belief that some sins were bigger, more serious, and more hell worthy than others. When I was living in the Bronx in the early seventies with my family, I made it a point to stay away from cursing, premarital sex, smoking, drinking, and the partying culture that was developing at that time. I made a conscious effort and deliberate decisions to live a godly, Christian life as I understood it. Of course, it made life lonely. When my classmates were enjoying themselves on Friday nights, I was at home.

I met Michael at church. He and his two navy buddies began attending our church. They were stationed in the Brooklyn Navy Yard. The friend that was responsible for them attending was married, and his father was a preacher in the denomination. The other friend was single and a body builder. When I first saw Michael, I felt he was there to pick up women and didn't much like him for that. Yes, I was quite judgmental. I think that's one side effect of very religious people. Like most churches, men were scarce, so when three men showed up, all available females were attentive. I was barely seventeen and not interested. I had plans. However, shortly afterwards, the two single men gave their lives to the Lord, Pentecostal style. It was after that when Michael and I began to date. I think he asked my father if he could date me. My father, as was the common belief of all good Christians, believed it was better to date someone "in the Lord" than to become "unequally yoked" with unbelievers. Michael was given permission. Make no mistake, by then it was okay with me. A year later, he asked my father for my hand in marriage and was again granted permission. My pastor and I talked as well. I remember him saying something like, "You can always go to college, but a good man doesn't come along every day." I was eighteen and he was twenty-three when we got married.

We went to church every week. I was at church whenever the doors opened. I went to Monday night prayer, Tuesday night Bible study, and we were at church all day Sunday. I couldn't sing so I couldn't sustain Wednesday night choir rehearsal. I was an usher and at one time served the pastor his liquid beverage during Sunday service. I was careful who was in our circle of friends, even if they were churchgoers. I had set my boundaries for my life, and drugs were not even a thought part of it. You can just imagine my shock and dismay when Michael told me he had been taking drugs—and crack of all things. Even I had heard about the devastation this new drug had caused on people. How could this be? It was unbelievable! However, I believed him when he said he would quit. I believed him when he said he was in control. I wanted to believe, and I did!

After that conversation, nothing changed other than he wasn't hiding it as much anymore. He never smoked in front of me, but I now knew what he was doing when he left my presence to go to the bathroom and later in the basement of our home, or when he left the house all together. Shortly after our initial conversation where he confessed and I realized he couldn't, wouldn't, or didn't want to stop, I began to get scared. Fear makes me do things I ordinarily might not do—more on this later. We started to argue a lot. I think I thought I could now control the situation and make him behave in an acceptable way. I watched him like a hawk and responded to his behavior in ways that only exacerbated the situation. At some point, I told the girls. Although he did not want them to know, it was becoming difficult to hide. He didn't realize how much he had changed, visibly and behaviorally. At some point, our minister and church family began to suspect. When I was asked what was wrong, I didn't hide it. His behavior was becoming increasingly odd and uncharacteristic of him. He was visibly disappearing in front of all our eyes. When I was asked what was wrong, there was nothing else to say but that he was on drugs.

A short while after he first admitted his drug use to me, I began to look at our finances. I knew enough to know he had to pay for it somehow. All through our marriage, Michael had always handled the money. He paid the bills and attended to our savings and checking account. He was actually very good at it, and unlike many wives, I didn't have to take on that burden. This meant I did not monitor our finances. We discussed substantial purchases, either before or after the fact. We really didn't keep a lot of secrets where this was concerned. Well, I decided to take a look at our finances. I followed the money. As it turned out, Michael had emptied over $40,000 over a period of twelve to eighteen months on crack. That's as far back as I could find bank statements from his credit union account. Our savings was in his credit union. His credit union was located near his job and a distance from our home. Although it was a joint account, it was difficult for me to physically access that account. We purposely did not get an ATM card for this account because we wanted it to be difficult to access. Our regular checking account (and a small savings account) easily accessible via ATM, which was used to pay bills and live off of, was in a nearby local bank. At that time I didn't notice any unusual activities in these accounts.

When I saw he had spent over $40,000 unbeknownst to me, I panicked, and fear took over. I immediately took his name off some accounts I had so he could not access them and began to monitor our checking and savings accounts. I later realized Michael would go to the supermarket, make a two-dollar purchase, and take forty dollars out in cash using his ATM card. This occurred two to three times weekly and increased to two to three times a day. I spent a lot of time arguing with him, but it was like arguing with the wall. There was no reasoning with him. He was no longer Michael. He was a walking brick with only the ability to rationalize his drug behavior. He became quite adept at turning the tables and placing the focus on me. My response to his behavior often became the issue instead of his bad behavior. It was quite frustrating.

I remember praying real hard for God to deliver him. That didn't work. The church was praying, to no avail. Despite his addiction, Michael continued to attend church every Sunday. Sometimes I wished he would stop attending. It was embarrassing for me. He was a member of the praise team and played the saxophone. He stopped attending rehearsals but was one of the first ones to get on stage Sunday mornings. While everyone was standing in place, Michael stood out. His movements were not smooth but rather jittery and jumpy. He could not keep still. He often tried harder than necessary, and I think this was so he could look normal. This only made him stand out more. No one said anything. No one discussed it. No one held him accountable. I'm not sure anyone knew what to do. Eventually, the praise team leader, a dear friend of ours, told him to step down. He had become difficult and defiant and wouldn't practice the songs at home.

When he wasn't on stage or performing a solo, which they were still allowing him to do, he was sitting next to me on Sunday mornings nodding off. This was no longer the "I'm sleeping and fighting to stay awake" nods he used to do. This was now the sitting on the stoop strung out nod that screamed substance abuse. It was embarrassing! He was always sweating. His clothes hung on him like clothes on a rack. No one said anything to him. Everyone would ask me, "How is Michael doing?" with Michael right there in the building. One Sunday, we had to call the ambulance because he passed out at church. I was so scared. I was also secretly hoping this would be the end of it one way or another. I was always hoping it would end, one way or another.

Despite all this, there were times when we would almost pretend we were our old selves and would go to dinner. I'm not sure if this was an anniversary or a birthday, but one day we went to the harbor to have dinner. As we were walking around the area and talking, I noticed all the people we passed who looked like they had mental issues, drug issues, or some type of illness. They all looked like Michael, frail and sick. My heart broke for them and him and me. This is what he had become. This is what we had become.

By this time, the girls had started coping in their own way. They were clinging to anything they could (not so much God). One daughter was an emotional wreck. Her only saving grace was she didn't live in the same state, so she didn't have to look at it all the time. One daughter who had kidney issues got worse. She carried her grief and pain in her body. Her health began to deteriorate. The third daughter began to display disturbing social behaviors while making very poor personal choices. She eventually moved away as well. Michael's struggle with drugs were as much a surprise to the girls as it was to me. He was about fifty years old, much too old to become addicted to crack for the first time. While he had not always made the best personal choices, nothing he did that we were aware of should have led to this. This was a man who loved his girls and showed it by how he acted. He was the one who took them to all their events. He was the one who made sure they got what they wanted when it was time to shop for school clothes. He was the "yes" parent. They loved him. It was hard for them to reconcile the man they were seeing with the dad they had always known.

Our family was crumbling in front of me, and I had no power to stop it. Oh, lest I forget, I was gaining weight steadily. I wore black every day. My wardrobe was void of colors. I developed diabetes and was taking quite a few pills to keep it under control. I was becoming devoid of emotions. I was an elementary school principal of a large school, a very stress-filled job. I went to work every day. I learned to leave my personal problems at home, embrace and deal with my job problems during work, only to pick back up my home problems when I reached the door of my house. I did this for the years we struggled with this issue. During this time, I told no one on the job. I feared the ramification of a drug-addicted spouse of a person who worked around children. He was no longer allowed to come to my job. I couldn't risk anyone finding out. I couldn't risk anyone looking at him and figuring it out. I worried about losing credibility if they found out. I worried about them losing respect for me. I was worried, I was scared, and I felt alone.

This doesn't mean I didn't try to reach out for help. I did. The praise team leader I mentioned told me about a church in another state that had a big deliverance ministry. She said they dealt with these types of issues all the time. I contacted them. I remember the minister to whom I spoke asking me what my church had done. I felt quite stupid but couldn't tell him anything that had been done for Michael or me. He told me he would have the minister in charge of this type of ministry contact me. I'm still waiting to hear from him. On those occasions when my pastor or one of the elders at my church would wait until Michael was out of earshot to ask me how he was doing, and I told them, I would hear, "You should leave him. He won't change until he hits rock bottom." I later found out a minister's wife had a brother who struggled with drugs, and another church sister had an ex-husband who struggled with crack. They never said anything!

We had been married for over twenty-five years. I didn't know anything else. Leaving was not where my mind was. I was still praying for a miraculous deliverance. I was secretly hoping Michael would wake up one morning and have no interest in smoking crack. I was "believing God for his healing and deliverance." One minute I was the believing Christian. The next minute I was a scared little girl who saw no end to the nightmare. When I was in the latter mood, I would degrade him with demeaning words. I heard fowl four-letter words leave my lips that would have made my mother cringe in her grave. Words like these didn't come from saved lips, but they came from mine. I felt hemmed in, pinned with walls all around me. I felt I had nowhere to go. I saw no help on any side of me. The only place I could look that didn't make me feel blocked in was up.

I remember thinking after a while that I had better take over the finances. Michael made it clear this was going to be a fight. He was not ready to give up control of the money and his ability to buy crack whenever he wanted, which by now was daily. I recall the day, I believe it was a Saturday, and he left as usual. I went down to the basement, which was now his man cave and personal crack spot. I fell on my knees and began to pray. I was crying with snot coming from me. I called out to the Lord. I remember telling the Lord I was scared and didn't know what to do. I didn't want to lose everything. Surprisingly, God responded. This was not the only time God responded to my cries during this ordeal. Every time I mentioned something I didn't want to lose, like my house, I heard the Lord say, "I'll buy you another one!" Or, I'm going to lose my car. He said, "I'll replace it!" His voice in my head was calm and rational and matter of fact. He reminded me He was the one who had gotten us everything we had and He would replace it if needed. I was told to leave the finances alone and let Michael continue to handle it. I knew it was God because my rational mind knew that drug use meant loss of everything, criminal activity, and possibly jail. Although I knew I heard God and although I got up from my knees that day with an assurance does not mean I listened. I decided I hadn't really heard from God and was going to do what was the wise thing to do.

I told Michael I would handle the finances. By now, of course, Michael was ready to admit he was not in control of his drug use. When we spoke calmly, he seemed to respond reasonably, initially. He still continued his behavior. He was an addict. Michael agreed to let me handle the bills. He had a certain amount of money he could use for whatever he wanted and was not allowed to dip in and take more. I paid the bills for about four to five months. Every time I paid the bills, something went wrong. I wound up over-drafting or doing something that would cost us money in the end. It was not Michael; it was me. After about four months of frustration, I turned the bills back over to Michael. Our mortgage was never late when Michael handled the bills. We owed nothing. Nothing was repossessed. During this ordeal, the only time we had banking issues resulting in financial loss was during the time I took over the bills. I decided to be obedient and trust I heard God.

Throughout this period, believe it or not, he went to work daily. Whether or not he remained at work once he got there, I don't know. He held his job. I can't explain that, but he did. On Saturdays, he would disappear for most of the day and return as high as a kite and as sweaty and stinky as a pig. This drug seemed to come through his pores as a noxious, offensive odor. Even on those rare occasions when he showered, he couldn't seem to wash the odor away. I don't have a keen sense of smell. However, I couldn't make that claim when it came to the odor that came from him. I also noticed his crack use came with an insatiable sexual appetite. Michael had always enjoyed sex and like most men never got enough. This was different. It was almost as though crack and sex went together like dessert after dinner. This was especially difficult for me. I had no idea what Michael was doing. I figured he was going to crack houses when he left the house for long periods of time and found out later he was. I just didn't know what else he was doing at the crack house besides smoking crack. I became concerned about my health, particularly contracting AIDS. For a while, I started to say no to his sexual demands. I didn't want to catch anything. I truly didn't want to die of AIDS. I remember battling the tapes in my head. "The wife's body belongs to her husband," and so on. I decided those scriptures were not meant for situations like these. Condoms were not a part of our sexual vocabulary. After twenty-five years, insisting on him using condom was like starting World War III. So I stopped having sex. He would come home and beg and plead, telling me he wasn't getting it anywhere else. I recall talking to God about it. I was making my argument that He couldn't expect me to knowingly and carelessly put my life in danger. Again,

God responded. I find it interesting that He couldn't respond to Michael's deliverance but could respond when it came to me putting my life in His hands. He told me He would protect me and I wouldn't catch anything. I grudgingly submitted my body to my crack-addicted husband, like a garbage disposal to garbage. I angrily and painstakingly obeyed what I heard.

Sometimes I feel like I was sacrificed for Michael. These were not the only times when God addressed my conduct instead of the obvious sinful behavior of my husband. One day after an argument and Michael leaving the house, I went to the basement to pray. I think I felt if I prayed in the basement where he smoked, I was not relinquishing control of our home to the enemy. Anyway, I was on my knees again, crying with snot running from my nose. I was complaining about Michael's bad and sinful behavior, asking God to deliver him. We had just argued about his drug habit and behavior. I remember using a string of four-letter words at him during the argument. I really surprised myself. You must understand. I didn't curse. I don't even say the word "cuss" because it sounds too much like I'm cursing. I lived my entire life not using foul language and staying away from anyone who did. I didn't realize how well I knew those words. They flowed so easily. So when Michael stormed out of the house after pointing at me and saying, "You are the problem!" I went to God out of frustration and guilt (I had now sinned). Once again, instead of focusing on Michael's deliverance, God decided to address my conduct. At first I really wasn't feeling Him. I began to give rebuttals. However, before long, God showed me a glimpse of Michael through His eyes. After I apologized to God for my conduct, I began to pray for Michael. I was no longer praying for my husband. I was praying for my brother in Christ.

God showed me the depth of love Michael needed. God did not look at him through eyes of disgust, contempt, and disappointment, like I did. Instead, I saw God's unconditional love and commitment to him. He showed me how fragile he was and the importance of him receiving unconditional love from me. It broke my heart. I had to become God to Michael. I believe that was the first time since our marriage that I was crystal clear on the depth of God's love toward each of us. Seeing Michael as my brother, I prayed for him and his specific needs without consideration for myself. It was suddenly not about me. It was all about him. This was so liberating and brought such clarity. I recall apologizing to Michael for my conduct the next day. The Lord began to teach me how to pray for my brother. I began to ask the Lord to send a man to walk alongside my brother so he could be delivered.

I recall another day when I was praying in the basement. I was feeling overwhelmed. Our house had been a model home for the builders prior to us buying it. When we purchased the house, it had not yet made it to the open market. We literally drove by, saw it, and I loved it. Our realtor made an appointment to visit, and the day we did, we made an offer. The builders intended to put it on the market that day. We bought it, and the house never made it to the open market. Well, my dream house had begun to show signs of wear and tear. On top of all the other things going on, the basement wall was cracked. We had been in the house about four to five years. We had a terrible snowstorm that year, and when the snow started to melt, our basement began to flood. Thank God our warranty was still in effect. We got everything fixed without any cost to us. Anyway, as I was saying, I was in the basement praying about Michael and our situation. It seemed like our situation consumed my prayer life. As I knelt there crying with snot coming from my nose, God shared something profound with me. He told me just like our house, there was a crack in our foundation. I didn't know if He specifically meant Michael or our marriage, or both. He said, just like the builders of our house who know the house and can fix it without any problems, He knew our house (He knew Michael and me). He was the only one that could fix the foundation. He took time during that prayer to walk me through an analogy that was quite profound. It was soothing and very encouraging. He helped me to see that it was all going to work out. That exchange made me realize this was a spiritual battle and the Lord was going to win. Michael could submit or not. It could be easy or it could be hard, but God was going to see it through. Just like the actual house foundation, God was going to knock down Michael's walls and rebuild his foundation. I can say, years later, He did!

This ordeal was a day-by-day struggle for all of us. Just because I got clarity one day does not mean I kept that clarity for long. The truth is I wavered back and forth between operating from a place of love and a place of fear. I believe love became stronger and fear weakened. Love eventually won. Eventually, Michael agreed to go to rehab. I can't recall how that came about. I believe the pastor, our girls, and I met with him, but I'm really not sure. It's amazing how some events are so imprinted in my memory, and others are like shadows, elusive. This is one such event. All I remember is when he decided to go to rehab, which his health insurance paid for, he was to go for about three months. I was so hopeful. His ticket was bought for him. Everything was set. The day we went to the airport, Michael was a little reluctant. As a matter of fact, we were in the airport waiting for him to board. He became increasingly agitated. Just before he boarded the plane, he turned around, said he was not going, and we returned to the house. I was so disheartened. I was livid! That was it! I was done! Enough! After a talk with the rehab center counselor, a new airline reservation was made. I didn't take him to the airport. I recall telling him I didn't care what he did. I was through! Michael entered rehab. I later found out the reason he returned to the house was because he had some leftover crack he wanted to smoke before going to rehab. He did not want it waiting for him when he returned home.

By the time Michael agreed to go to rehab, my family and his family were fully aware of the problem. I don't think my family believed me. One sister lives near us. The rest of my siblings lived in other states. I don't think they could imagine Michael on drugs. I think it defied their imaginations. I sometimes think they believed I must have done something or it was my fault, or my exaggerated imagination. I don't think they fully got it. Then one day, some of them came for a visit and saw him. They immediately knew something was wrong. However, to this day, I'm not sure they comprehended the severity of his addiction.

Michael's family, on the other hand, eventually realized he was in trouble. One of his sisters made herself available and became his confidant. She listened to him and, I assumed, advised him. I don't know what I expected them to do, but needless to say, no one lived up to my expectations. Oh well! I began to get a glimmer of hope when his family came to visit us one holiday. His mother, who doesn't fly, his father, and his brothers came. They surrounded him with no recriminations. They saw the way he looked, and there was no mistake; Michael was in real trouble. It was shortly after that when Michael went to rehab.

Rehab was not well received by Michael. When we talked by phone, he would tell me how all they seemed to talk about was alcoholism and he was not an alcoholic. He participated in their counseling sessions and activities but remained a bit resistant. When it was time for the family visit, I went. Shortly after my visit, I got a call that Michael was trying to leave rehab against counsel. Michael left rehab after six weeks. Michael came home and entered an outpatient clinic but about nine months later relapsed and resumed his drug activity. I was disheartened! My hopes were dashed, and I was now giving serious thought to leaving him.

After leaving rehab, Michael and I sought out a male psychologist that he could talk to. He had positive things to say about the counseling sessions while he was in rehab. He also took the advice of the rehab counselors and started attending

AA meetings. I attended some with him. Michael kept saying he didn't need to attend AA meetings. He felt they didn't address his needs. I became scared and concerned again. My life now became that of watcher. I spent my days and nights terrified. Every time he left my sight, I was terrified he was going to start using again. He did. However, he continued to see the counselor and attend some meetings. I was still asking God to send him the right man (male person) to walk with him. I was also trying to take control of my life. I began to wonder if he would ever get clean. I wasn't sure I wanted to stick around and find out years later I was still in the same place.

It was around this time that Michael met Greg. I believe Greg was the person God sent to help Michael walk out his deliverance. Greg was a long-time recovering addict. He fully got Michael. I remember him meeting with Michael and me in the basement and telling me to give him some time. He was going to help Michael through this. He genuinely liked Michael and was impressed with him. There was not a hint of disdain for Michael, and he was not repelled by the addiction. After a while, he and Michael agreed it was time to return to rehab. This time he went to one that was driving distance from our house. After five days, Michael came home.

Five days of rehab did not impress me. If he couldn't stay clean after a month of rehab, how was he going to stay clean after five days? I realized with God all things were possible but for years I'd been waiting for the possible that hadn't come. I became scared again, and I began to look for an apartment.

I found a cute little one-bedroom and was beginning to get excited about the prospect of living on my own for the first time in my life. I was also a little bit scared. It was days from Christmas. I resigned myself to the upcoming change and settled my mind into what was coming. I decided to spend a few days with a friend. I packed a bag. I don't recall if I even told Michael

I was leaving for a few days. I left, hoping he would notice and realize he didn't want to live without me and come to his senses. Day two of my stay with my friend and sister, I heard the Lord say, "Go home! And be quiet!"

As always, I questioned what I heard. However, I quickly packed up a few things and told my friend I was leaving. I think she thought I was coming back. I didn't say anything because I expressly felt "be quiet" meant "stop talking so much." I was talking quite a bit to her, complaining and hashing things out, praying and crying, just making noise.

When I got home, Michael was home. He was on our king- size bed sprawled out in warmth and luxury. I, on the other hand, had just spent the night in a cold apartment, in an uncomfortably small bed. I became angry. I started to ask myself, why do I have to leave my home? Why does he get to stay and enjoy what we've worked so hard for? I decided I was going to listen to God, and I stayed. I called the apartment complex and told them to disregard my application. By now I was quite angry. Michael did not seem to notice I was gone. He didn't seem to care. I think I said something sarcastic about his attitude. He mentioned that he didn't tell me to leave and didn't want me to leave. We eventually started to talk.

As the new year approached, I stopped taking and making phone calls. I was being obedient. God continued to talk with me. I remember He said, He was "hiding me from Satan." That was the first time I truly understood that God's enemy was not God. He was not all seeing, all knowing, all consuming. He could not occupy all space at all times. The concept of "hiding me" was further revealed to me as the opportunity for the enemy to stop thinking or focusing on me. God also told me that things would change after the new year—new year, new beginning. Michael, my friend, and I went to dinner New Year's eve. Michael and I went on to visit a church and brought in the new year at church.

As we drove home New Year's day, God continued to impress on me the fact that it was over. After all these years, the drug ordeal had ended as suddenly as it had begun. As I look back, I recall two occasions other than the ones already mentioned where my conversations with God were noteworthy. We were at church on Sunday during the praise and worship portion of the service. I don't recall the specific song we were singing. All I recall is the fact that during that song, God gave me a glimpse of what He had done in heaven. He had released the angels and dispatched them on Michael's behalf. I lost it. I know everyone must have looked at me like I was crazy. Our church was a toned down evangelical type church. Very few practiced a prayer language openly, and emotional displays were not shown too often. That day, they got an earful and an eyeful. I didn't care!

There was another instance during this ordeal when I was home alone. Michael had gone where Michael went in those days. I was lying on my bed watching TV and feeling very sorry for myself and my predicament. I was despondent but thoughtful. I remember thinking how happy the enemy was to have me in a place of feeling defeated. He had shut my mouth. I was not praising God anymore! I was defeated. I recall speaking scriptures to myself. I began to encourage myself with the word. Before I knew it, I was up, out of bed, and on my feet walking around declaring my love for God. I did something a bit foolish. I began to challenge the enemy. I told him, "Bring it on!" I told him the more Michael used drugs, the more I was going to praise God. All the days of my appointed time I would praise the Lord! I remember preaching the goodness of God to myself. I called Him by His descriptive names. By the time I ended, I was changed. God was getting the glory from my situation. I was no longer feeling sorry for myself. I was doing what I was born to do, praise and worship!

By the time the journey was over, I was a changed believer. I was no longer self-righteous and judgmental, or at least not so much. I enjoyed an intimate relationship with the Lord versus the dutiful relationship we had. By the time this journey ended, I was asking God to let me breathe His breath, exhale after He inhales, to let me finish his sentences. I envisioned lying on his chest and being so in sync you couldn't tell who was inhaling and who was exhaling. I recall another conversation with God where I thanked Him for the experience and told Him I would not change a thing. When the words came out of my mouth, I surprised myself. I remember the conversation we had where God called me "faithful." He explained faithful was not that we get it right all the time. Faithful was getting back up after being knocked down. Faithful was going through the motions day after day after day even when you don't feel like it. Faithful is not giving up. I smiled that day.

As I end my portion of the story, I must say, as much as the journey deepened my relationship with God, the journey left me a bit scarred, and Michael and my relationship a bit fragile. Like him, I was wounded. It took some time to heal. At some point, I had to make a conscious decision to forgive him and give myself permission to take the time I needed to heal. It's been a little over eight years since the ordeal ended. I am finally wearing colors again. I have lost some weight, with medical assistance. I am mostly healed and can hardly see the scars. Michael and I are doing well. The girls are well. God has given us a chance to help them heal. We are blessed with a grandson and a granddaughter. I can now share my testimony with the world.

# CHAPTER 13
• • • • • • • • • • • • •
## Securing the Peace within Me

I SPOKE EARLIER ABOUT THE VARIOUS jobs I held in my youth that set the beginning stages for my work ethic. Shortly after my discharge from the navy in 1975 and while collecting unemployment benefits, it was still unclear to me what my career choice would be. At the time, I believed my only talent or skill was in music. However, this was not enough because I still lacked an in-depth knowledge in music theory, which I would have obtained if I had remained in college. Although I had a desire to continue pursuing music, I thought it would be a disservice to my wife and future family to pursue such an unpredictable career choice. So I began seeking employment, and while doing so, a door was opened for me to interview for a job with the federal government. It was an entry-level job but offered a career path with benefits. The job was sponsored through the Veterans Administration where honorably discharged veterans were placed in government jobs to begin a career. The interview was for a communications specialist job. I was pleased by the outcome of the interview because they were interested in hiring me but couldn't at the time, until an employee in that position retired. I was told they were not sure when the employee would retire but would let me know as soon as the position became available.

In the interim, I wanted to work instead of collecting unemployment, especially while seriously considering an engagement with my future wife. I subsequently got a job working on Wall Street for a steamship company, as a freight cashier, making slightly higher than the minimum wage. After about three months working for company, I received a letter from the government's personnel office stating the communication's job I interviewed for was available and they would hire me if I was still interested. It didn't take long to accept this offer because I had already envisioned the potential career growth within the government. I was hired through a program called Veterans' Readjustment Appointment (VRA), which provided assistance for Vietnam veterans to obtain full employment. I began working for the federal government (NOAA) in 1975 at the age of twenty-three, a few weeks after getting married. It was exciting to start a new job with obvious financial security and extra benefits such as sick leave, annually leave, and paid holidays. My starting salary was more than I had previously made, and the benefits were much better.

My job was located in Rockefeller Center, a national historic landmark located in the heart of Manhattan. This one building stands seventy fl oors, including NBC Studios, an observation deck at the very top, and the famous Rainbow Room, which offers exquisite dining and entertainment on the sixty-fifth floor. As equally appealing, its surroundings were spectacular with the skating rink in front during season of iconic ice, acclaimed Radio City Music Hall across the street, and a banquet of shops, specialty stores, dining halls, massive sculptures, and public art displays. The weather service where I worked was located on the mezzanine floor of Rockefeller Plaza, which probably covered a huge square footage of space. The office spaces included a climatology department, weather marine unit, communications area, weather radar operations, an area for aviation/public forecasting, and other administrative offices. After completing school, my goal was to move up from communications to actually forecasting weather, and I did. I worked at this office fifteen years and performed in nearly every position within the office spaces we occupied. Working for the weather service was the first job I ever had where I actually began to think about a path for my career and future. During the first six months on the job, I knew I had a future with this agency and envisioned the unlimited possibilities. I quickly learned my assigned duties and responsibilities and was pleasantly surprised when my supervisor and other high-level employees commented how well I performed my job. They went as far as saying I was the best communicator they had seen, including those who had worked in that position for many years. Within a couple years, I had received commendations and awards not given to many. Being mentally in that space was certainly gratifying and uplifting and helped me to see myself unlike I had ever seen or experienced during my life up to that point. The sensation of that accomplishment made me feel good about myself, which triggered positive responses from coworkers and gave me a sense of satisfaction I rarely obtained. Growing up in an environment where getting a college education seemed distant and unimportant led me to have low expectations and go down a path with un-thought-out consequences. It was not until I reached the age of twenty-five that I actually began to set goals for myself and started to chart a deliberate course for my future. This particular job opened my eyes to see and envision the possibilities and allowed me to leave my comfort zone and to think bigger.

## Getting the Job Done

After two years on the job I gained confidence in my ability to accomplish any task I put my mind to do. A consolation of this was when my boss, the meteorologist in charge of the office, took me to the side and encouraged me to pursue meteorology. I was surprised and somewhat stunned when he said to me that by the time I ended my career, I should retire at his pay grade or higher. He was almost at the top of the government's general schedule (GS) pay grade. This was especially eye-opening because I was at the bottom of the pay schedule. Whether he realized it or not, he influenced me to set higher goals for my career than I would have if we never spoke.

I was twenty-five years old before I seriously began to examine my station in life. I decided to pursue meteorology. Until then, music had been my sole interest, and I, quite frankly, had considered nothing else. After two years of working in communications, I began to envision how I could move up through the ranks within the agency. At one point, I thought about pursuing cartography, but it was obvious meteorology was the best choice considering the clear path by working in that particular office. I knew, in order to meet this goal, I had to go back to school and obtain a degree in meteorology. With this in mind, there were obviously other things I had to consider while making this choice. I thought about how I would maintain my employment while attending college and knew it would be hard work. I also knew it would take a commitment on my part to finish. Another consideration was the fact I had begun raising a family and made barely enough money to sustain my wife, two kids, and one other child on the way. However, I was mentally prepared for the challenge and decided it could be done. I also figured I needed to be close to home. My job was in Manhattan, but I lived in Queens, which presented a small but less important challenge. There were several colleges nearby in Queens I could attend, but none offered a degreed program in meteorology. The only school offering a curriculum in meteorology was City College located in Upper Manhattan about an hour from home. Because I wanted to be close to home, I made the decision to begin my studies at York College, only minutes away from where I lived. My plans included transferring to City College before declaring my major. I also had to consider whether to take day or evening classes. I knew evening classes would limit my choices and my ability to carry the required courses I needed, so I settled for day classes. Day classes, I thought, would not only allow me to take the required courses but also enable me to carry a course load as a full-time student. I started college in 1977, and each year of college, I carried a minimum of twelve credits per semester while working the midnight shift and raising a young family.

I was fortunate to be a veteran because the VA paid my tuition under the infamous GI Bill. This helped supplement my, then, meager income but could only be maximized if I carried a full load. The extra money was a blessing, but school and work were very exhausting. I was also fortunate enough to have a job that permitted me to work the nightshift when necessary while attending college during the day. When I left work, I went straight to school, sometimes not reaching home until late evening. I averaged about four hours of sleep before returning to work that night. This particular pinch required a lot of hard work and sleepless nights, a sacrifice I had to make to meet my goal. As with most plans, things don't necessary work out quite as we anticipate. I had to make a few adjustments along the way. After about three years at York College, I had taken my required electives, physics, chemistry, math, and a few geology courses. At this juncture, I began preparing for my major studies and to make the transfer to City College. But as I assessed my situation, I realized I could kill two birds with one stone by simultaneously, attending both colleges because they were both part of the City University of New York (CUNY), and I could attend City College as a permit student. This allowed me to study geology at York College and meteorology at City College. The circumstances were such that both geology and meteorology had nearly the same science prerequisites for their degreed programs. I spent another three years before I completed my required course work in these two major fields of study and graduated 1983. It was six grueling years of hard work, sacrifices, and dedication to complete college. There were many times when I felt the urge to quit while enduring the challenge of working forty hours weekly and carrying a full load, but I persevered and finished school.

## Peace through work experience

As stated earlier in the book, throughout my early

childhood and adolescence, my self-image was impacted by many unfortunate circumstances. In addition, my own internalization of who I was and the thought of my potential was nonsexist. I soon began to realize my past thinking was shortsighted, unintentional, and damaging to my overall worth as a human being. As I began to think introspectively, I understood and realized how I had sabotaged and poisoned my potential through unproductive thinking. This was a life-changing experience, but I knew there were obviously mental and psychological obstacles I still needed to overcome. Working in a science, structured environment and personally seeing, for the first time, professional scientists do their jobs well at work was a boost to my self-esteem and increased my self-awareness. My self-esteem was heightened through the constant encounters with men and women who took their jobs seriously and who seemed to embody the type of work ethics I had never experienced. They also appeared to project the confidence and stability in the work environment conducive to a cohesive unit. My self- awareness was raised through observing how they performed their jobs and how they understood the fundamentals of the job's requirement.

Over many years, I had created self-inflicted barriers through the lack of confidence in myself and built up insecurities stemming from a relatively troubled childhood. As I watched and observed my coworkers, the majority of whom were Caucasian, I realized I possessed the same faculties as they to competently accomplish any task. There was no mistake. I had reached a crossroad in my life, and I was determined to address the insecurities and past misguided thinking. When I completed my formal education in meteorology and began to compete with other employees, I clearly recognized the inherent biases within the office quarters where I worked. While advancing through the ranks, there were interns whom I trained competing for the same positions. There were occasions, during evaluations, when some of those same interns received higher marks than I did when I knew they were not as efficient as I. On one particular evaluation, my supervisor talked as if I were at the top of the evaluation scale, but on paper, my evaluation was in the middle range. His comments appeared to be disingenuous and contradictory. When this occurred, I walked away with anger and discouragement. But after giving it some thought, I returned the next day and expressed my feelings in a constructive way. To my surprise, he changed my evaluation, which reflected his rhetoric. There were several other instances where I felt unfairly judged and frustrated by the actions from members of my peer group of meteorologists. After completing my studies in college and as I began to compete with others vying for forecasting slots, I realized how disadvantaged I was in getting the positions I sought. Even as an intern, at one point there were about three others whom I would compete with for forecast slots. Out of the four of us, I would receive the least amount of training, which diminished my chances of getting a forecast position. By this time, I had exceeded all the prerequisites and necessary qualifications to do the job of a forecaster but was denied an opportunity to train with veteran forecasters. Being the only African American on staff and experiencing the disparate treatment, whether intentional or unintentional, I felt discouraged, excluded, and undervalued as an employee. On several occasions, I was compelled to speak with my boss to rectify the training discrepancies.

My overall experience during the first fifteen years being employed by NOAA was positive, but I had to be more aggressive than others to get into the positions I thought I deserved. Over time, I requested and was given additional program leader assignments, which included work in the weather marine program where I set up ship contacts to supply the office critical information. I served as the offices' Weather Service evaluation officer working with the Federal Aviation Administration (FAA) toward ensuring their flight service personnel met national standards through inspections and training. I performed disaster preparedness duties while working closely with emergency managers and providing training to volunteers for weather assistance. And I served as the office satellite focal point, where I was a resource to forecasters involving new satellite technology. I accepted these extra duties to help the office and to place myself in a position of strength as far as job advancements was concerned. I was gaining peace through experience.

## Moments of Satisfaction and Prosperity

My extra hard work paid off. Through these additional assignments and work growth, I was promoted to work at one of NOAA's weather service's regional headquarters in 1990. After fifteen years of shift work, my new job's assignment took me out of the field environment of forecasting and gave me a different perspective of NOAA. I was now a program manager and policy maker, managing huge observing programs and overseeing hundreds of local offices, covering fifteen to twenty different states within this one region.

Working in this capacity gave me a perspective of how policies affect both the regional and local field offices differently. I realized there was a distinct and prevalent mentality at both office levels, where the local office would recoil from policies developed by the regional office, and in response, the regional office would push back harder because they could not understand why; their policies, to them, made perfect sense. I could clearly see both sides and understood the distance and misunderstandings between the two from having worked in both the local and regional environments. While working out of the local forecast office, I recall many occasions where the regional office would develop policies that didn't make much sense to the local office staff, including myself, who had to carry them out. To the local office, these policies appeared to be too broad to function effectively. On the other hand, once I began work at the regional office, I understood their challenge in making policies that covered huge territories and different climate boundaries, which from their perspective made sense. The region's objective was to make the local offices work better, but in some cases, it was a bad fit for some local offices within the regional coverage. Furthermore, in some instances, the regional office would be bound by certain policies developed by the NWS national headquarters. Each would have a legitimate argument but, in many cases, failed to communicate in a way that would blend complete understanding of what was required and appropriate for each entity. As the regional's observing program manager, these were challenges I also faced working out of the regional office while interfacing with both the local office and national headquarters, where I tried my best to bridge the gaps.

This job afforded me the opportunity to travel to many states within the continent to conduct inspections, attend conferences, and participate in various utility training sessions. Considering my background and humble beginnings, as a young kid having very little, I was grateful to have reached this position in my career and at peace with my station in life. It was certainly an accomplishment and sweet place to be at that time of my life. However, my experience working at the regional office was varied with ups and downs, just as the cycles of living in an imperfect world. Before I left regional headquarters, I was appointed the regional's Next Generation of Radars (NEXRAD) program manager but had to maintain the observing programs until someone else was hired into the position. This situation was troubling and burdensome because it lasted for nearly six months. Doing both job functions became a burden and almost impossible to manage for that lengthy period. It was especially problematic because the radar's job was a newly created position carrying a huge learning curve. Although I spoke up about the difficulty of continuing to perform my old job and the new one, no one appeared to have seen the urgency as I did, even though the local offices were being deprived of a dedicated person to oversee these huge programs. I carried the load of working two different jobs over a five-month period, considerably above the average workload of many other office workers, but I never received an appreciable acknowledgment of the work I did. It became disconcerting and frustrating, especially when observing others receive accolades and awards for simply doing their jobs. The thought of my not being rewarded for the work I was doing didn't affect my work ethic because I enjoyed doing my job and performed the best I could despite the prevailing distractions before me.

Before leaving the region, I applied for a couple of job openings for forecast office managers but was not chosen. I was even told by a supervisor she didn't think I was ready for the job. I didn't beg to differ because that was her opinion and she was the selecting official. I realized it was also her prerogative to place people into positions where she thought they would be a good fit. This was not new to me because I had noticed that people tended to underestimate my abilities for some reason or another. I refused to dwell on my troubled circumstances but pressed on to live for better times. I didn't realize it, but, at the time, I was in fact living in peace while simultaneously living in pieces. This perspective made it easy for me to endure the mental discomfort but enjoy the satisfaction of having a job. Ultimately she selected and approved me to become, I believe, the first African American to hold a new important key meteorology position in the weather service. In retrospect, working at our regional headquarters was a gift to me and helped to shape my future career with NOAA.

## Career Path on Course

I moved to Charleston, West Virginia, in 1994 to work out of a local weather office as the meteorologist who would be the primary face for the local office. This job was most fulfilling because I was able to travel throughout most of the state as well as other parts of Virginia, Ohio, and Kentucky. The most affirming part of my work as a government servant was not only being in a position to assist forecasters and other staff members with the resources they needed but also ensuring that good relations between the office and the outside community was maintained. Working for the weather service in Charleston was another mixed bag of experiences I do not regret having. When I began the job, I had a clear conscience of purpose because all those special and extra duties I had performed during my employment in New York were part of this particular job's responsibilities. As the meteorologist coordinator, I was the office go-to person regarding policies, office programs, and the outreach activities. The highlights of this job were meeting with various community groups and public officials and actively leading hundreds of weather training sessions. These were the folks our office worked closely with and who provided us the support to do our jobs.

My first decision was to meet every single emergency manager under the umbrella of our forecast warning area, which included sixty-six counties. I made a schedule and spent two months of my new job on the road, meeting each emergency manager, which proved to be very productive. For example, I worked closely with emergency managers and the media to change the old Emergency Broadcast System (EBS) to the now existing Emergency Alert System (EAS). Through this effort and many others, our office enjoyed strong public and private sector partnerships. I had also previously worked with the aviation community through conducting pilot weather briefing inspections and flight services. With this background and knowledge, I was among many other meteorologists privileged to participate in the government-sponsored familiarization flight program. This was a cooperative program developed between the government and the aviation administration where forecasters were allowed to ride in the jump seat of a plane's cockpit with pilots. I took several of these flights and regarded them to be very educational. I was able to experience, firsthand, what pilots do and see during a typical flight. The program was discontinued after the September 11 terrorist attacks, but the experience flying in the jump seat of a plane was a delight. These and many other positive memories will stay with me forever. I also worked rotating shifts, filling in for leave and absences when needed, and provided overall staff supervision in the absence of the office's boss.

One interesting and fulfilling aspects of my job was the occasion to participate in career fairs or what was formally called career days. I had participated in several career fairs in New York and didn't feel it was unfamiliar territory when asked to participate at schools in West Virginia. My previous participation in career fairs required each professional to set up a table and give out pertinent workplace pamphlets. The participants would also answer questions from the students as they moved about, in a large open space, to view career information provided by the participants. However, my first participation in a career fair in West Virginia was different from those I was accustomed to. When I reached the school, the first thing the career coordinator addressed was the career fair's format. Unlike the other career fairs I had done, this one required the participant to move from room to room to speak about his or her profession. I was not mentally prepared for this kind of recital because I hadn't developed talking points for this type of situation. I, of course, knew my profession and meteorology well and how to talk about it, but this format was simply new to me. I had to think fast about what I would say to the students for a half hour, the time we were allowed to talk in each classroom. I immediately drew on my personal experience before I decided to become a meteorologist. I thought about all the important but careless decisions I made before making meteorology a choice. I thought about how I had not given thought to or set any kind of goals, even though I had been taught and told many times how important it was to do, especially for my career path. And I thought about the many everyday choices and decisions we make without giving much thought to how they could impact the rest of our lives, no matter how big or small. This thought process raced through my mind before I was summoned to speak. By that time, I had developed my talking points and was ready to present my story. For every career fair thereafter, I talked about where I worked, the duties I performed, and what it takes to become a meteorologist. But I would also discuss, in a more practical sense, the importance of the choices and decisions we make every single day and how they impact our future. I would tie this discussion into the importance of setting career goals for a career path. I actually realized, through this experience, I had a wealth of knowledge from which to draw, and this exchange reminded me that my personal experiences are my own, and no one can take them away.

## Problems Don't Last Always

As with most workplace environments, there were a few serious personnel issues in our office, but when they surfaced, I was, in most instances, caught in the middle of assisting with office problems and disputes. For instance, a dispute developed between an office IT person and their supervisor, which I was not aware of until my boss asked for my advice. Without going into much detail, I was given pertinent information concerning the matter and gave my opinion where I thought the main problem rested. I believed the problem was exacerbated by the supervisor's lack of judgment and did not rest solely on the IT person. My boss agreed and accepted what I had to offer. I thought I had made my point and needed no further discussion, but it did not end there. What I didn't count on was that my boss would mention my name in his effort to resolve the issue. After he and the electronics supervisor discussed the matter, and because he agreed with me, I began to sense resentment toward me from the supervisor and one of her subordinates. By not initially realizing where the bitterness originated, I was somewhat baffled by their behavior until I discovered the longstanding office history between my boss and the supervisor, which had gone on years before I arrived at the office. On the face of it, I figured I had done nothing but simply offer an objective point of view about a serious issue confronting two staff members. Instead, I found myself embroiled in an unanticipated estrangement between myself and two other office employees with whom I, before then, enjoyed good relations. Despite their attitude and contempt toward me, I maintained a graceful response until one of them apparently sabotaged my computer's hard drive, which wiped out most of my files I had created over a year's time. I unashamedly confronted them both because they were the primary keepers of maintaining my computer. I was disturbed because of the inconvenience it caused and the seemingly outright disregard of proper decency by a professional. They were members of the IT staff and knew much more about computer issues than I but claimed the damage was done by accident. I had no proof and could not dispute their veracity but felt deeply that the act was done intentionally. It was very difficult for me to hold my tongue and not become resentful, but I gave them the benefit of the doubt and treated them as I had always done before. However, within the depths of my soul, I believe they committed the act willfully. Obviously they had a problem with me, but I was intent on not making their problem my problem and making a bad situation worse. My internal thought process, in this regard, has constantly guided my behavior, keeping me at a peaceful level even while enduring disappointments and conflicts. I showed no disrespect and conducted myself as I normally do, with civility and respect. As time passed, these same individuals exhibited an attitudinal 180-degree shift toward me.

As with most of my experiences on the job, reviewing my midterm and yearly evaluations always seemed to have a similar ring to it. During my evaluations, I would first hear what my supervisor had to say, but the results seemed to always be different on paper, which carried the real weight of any performance assessment. The job in Charleston was no different. My boss would always compliment me and tell me what a great job I was doing, but the actual evaluation would reveal less than the verbal assessments. Even though I was always told I did outstanding work, my counterpart seemed to receive better evaluations, and he obviously did less than I because I not only dealt with the public and media but also provided most of the staff support. By this time in my career, I had developed a keen understanding of the human unconscious bias. There is something about the unconscious nature in the way we think that eludes many. After working with and knowing my boss, I knew he was fair-minded and even a liberal thinker, but his assessment of my performance, compared to my other white counterparts, was always lacking. I'm convinced he could not see or discern his subconscious bias. I had witnessed this behavior many times before when it related to assessing minorities and women's job performance. With all that said and done, I still consider the job I occupied in West Virginia to be the best job I had during my entire weather service career.

## Adjunct Professor

I worked and served as an adjunct professor at the Beckley West Virginia College, where I taught an introductory meteorology course. This job required a great deal of initial work but added to my peace quotient. This opportunity was presented when the dean of the college approached my office, stating the college was losing their meteorology teacher and needed someone to teach the course until they were able to hire a permanent meteorologist. For the most part, most of our staff were degreed meteorologists and had the credentials to teach the course, but after canvasing staff members, no one had a desire or interest in teaching the course. From the dean's vantage point, it appeared to be an urgent matter, and she appeared to have exhausted all options other than eliminating the course, which the college did not want to do. After some consideration, I reluctantly accepted the challenge. My current job was already demanding a lot from me, but I felt the importance of keeping meteorology part of the college's program.

Teaching this course came with other specific challenges because the person before me left no previous class assignments or body of work to continue the course with continuity. He left nothing. I was forced to develop my own course syllabus. I taught two-hour classes twice a week while continuing my primary duties as a weather service employee. I taught for one semester while the college searched to recruit a permanent professor for the course. Teaching this course gave me a different outlook on teaching and true respect for teachers who spend their entire careers teaching. Of course, I was already familiar with the importance and extraordinary work teachers do in performing the job of teaching students because my wife had taught for many years and was currently an assistant principal at a junior high school in Charleston. My serving as an adjunct professor and teaching for that short period truly opened my eyes to the dedication it takes and energy teaching requires from an educator's point of view. I'm eternally grateful for having been allowed to teach and growing to have an even greater respect for the teaching profession.

# Approaching Career's Apex

In the late nineties, I received a temporary assignment as the weather service's liaison to NOAA, its parent agency. This assignment allowed me work with a strategic planning office in the District of Columbia. I provided clear communications for budgetary matters between the weather service and NOAA. After my temporary assignment was over, I was reassigned to a small weather service strategic planning unit at the weather service headquarters in Silver Spring, Maryland. This office was comprised of a small group of high-level employees assembled to develop specific long-term strategic plans for the weather service's future. I also served as the subject matter expert in meteorology programs, provided assistance with equal employment opportunity issues, and worked with diversity affairs. I had a lot of flexibility and worked closely with the weather service's Equal

Employment Opportunity Program Office and NOAA's Diversity Office. Although a meteorologist, I gained a tremendous amount of human resource skills while assisting these program areas and acquired considerable knowledge in workforce planning, training development, and facilitation. My facilitation training brought about many traveling opportunities. I traveled across the country facilitating small groups, helping them resolve sometimes long-standing office issues. I love to help people and have been instrumental in resolving the sometimes seemingly insurmountable obstacles people face.

This job also had its ups and downs. Even though I assisted various groups outside of my office purview, I often felt I didn't receive the credit I deserved from my supervisor. He appeared to have reservations about my potential and my capabilities, which seemed to have been a common experiential thread of doubt from past supervisors during the thirty-two years of my government service. Just like many before, my evaluations were average even when my labor would go above and beyond my primary scope of responsibilities. Ironically, I liked every one of my supervisors, and I never exhibited or had any ill feelings toward them. They were all white, and their dispositions concerning African Americans, I believe, had been tainted from a societal norm that tends to view people of color as having exceptional raw talent but lacking the same acuity of intellect as they do. These are simply my personal views and observations from many years in the workplace environment.

# CHAPTER 14
## • • • • • • • • • • • •
## Pieces Coming Together

I HAD THE DISTINGUISHED OPPORTUNITY to act and perform in a black history production, which brought about fond memories. I participated in a play conducted during Black History Month, which was outside my job responsibilities but rewarding. A pamphlet was placed throughout the building soliciting performers, musicians, and stage handlers. Being a musician, of course, it aroused my curiosity, and I signed up to participate in the skit. Very few people signed up, and those who did were asked to play more than one role. Although my interest was primarily to participate as a musician, I was asked to perform several parts of the play. The play was developed based on writings of Carter G. Woodson, an African American writer and historian who was known as the father of Black History Month. The play was called "A Stroll through Black History" depicting the plight of African American history from the times of slavery to the era of the civil rights movement. Prior to the premiere of the play, I accepted several parts, which included Booker T. Washington, Frederick Douglas, portrayal of Paul Robeson's version of "Old Man River," and performance as John Coltrane on the sax at the Cotton Club. I had never acted before except, as far as I can remember, when I performed in a few skits in elementary school. To be perfectly honest, participating in this play/musical of black history was the highlight of my experience at the Herbert Hoover building.

# Big's Local Chapter President

A few years prior to my retirement but not from an initial desire, I was elected president to represent the Blacks in Government (BIG) local chapter of NOAA. Blacks in Government is a nationwide organization established in 1975 to serve as an advocate for black government employees while promoting opportunities and fairness affecting the rights of these employees. I was approached on several occasions by a colleague and longtime member of BIG to join, but being a member did not interest me until her persistence wore me down and I eventually joined. After less than a year being a member, many members of the chapter pushed for me to become their president when the current president's term was up. Becoming the president of the chapter was the furthest thing from my mind, and I really didn't want to accept that type of responsibility. However, the insistence of many members convinced me to seek the office, but I must admit, I did reluctantly and was elected for a two-year term.

My presidency began with a few challenges from the start because, at the time, there were several other members who wanted a long-standing member to be president but did not have the votes. Most members felt she was not qualified or a good candidate to represent the local chapter. After the election, this fact caused a rift between members of the two camps. Her supporters felt she deserved the office because of her time as a member, her outspokenness, and my relatively new status as a member. The vice president and longtime member would have been an excellent choice to be president and would have undoubtedly been elected, but she had no interest in the position. Apparently she had been around long enough to understand the huge challenge of leading the chapter. The issue I faced would have been mute if she wanted the presidency. Ironically, she was instrumental in my becoming a member and one of the main people who pushed for me to seek the NOAA local chapter's presidency.

Suffice to say, I had to confront this issue head-on when I became president. My predecessor did a good job as president for many years but over time decided someone else needed to take the helm and lead the local chapter. The chapter was also well respected at the national level. When I became president, I made a promise and set a goal during my tenure to improve the chapter's visibility and credibility within NOAA. To meet these goals, my first steps were to increase the chapter's membership and meet with upper management within the NOAA structure. Within the first year of my tenure, I met with many high-ranking members of NOAA and personally sought and recruited several people I knew to become members of our local chapter. By the end of my first year, our local chapter's membership doubled through my efforts, along with other recruitment and promotional activities the chapter had established. In addition, I put in many hours assisting black members of NOAA with employment and management issues. The local chapter, under my leadership, took on civil rights and fairness issues that gained prominence within the NOAA cultural structure. I served the first two-year term and was elected a second two-year term shortly before I retired. Neither term was easy. There were several disgruntled members who were not satisfied no matter what I did, and there were issues, which seemed trivial to me, between my vice president and some committee chairs whom I appointed. Many of these issues were resolved before my second term ended, and I was fortunate to have served in this leadership's role.

# Beyond the Realms of Conscious Thought

Sometimes I believe peace comes through not remembering all of the bad or less relevant things in the past. It may appear to be irrelevant, but for some strange reason, I simply don't remember much of my childhood. I seem to be the only one in my family who cannot recall many of the events that occurred in our neighborhood during our youth. All of my siblings can vividly remember their childhood and have no problem recounting specific incidents even from an early age. I left St. Louis when I was a teenager and never returned to live there permanently, although I try to visit frequently because most of my family still lives there. Invariably, when I visit, my siblings and I sit around reminiscing about different events that took place while growing up. Virtually all of my brothers and sisters can systematically and sequentially remember things to the smallest details, even those that involve me. It's not like I don't remember anything, because I can recall some major events that took place, but my memory seems to be clouded, mainly when trying to recall the names of people who grew up in our neighborhood. It is also hard for me to remember certain events that took place and some of the scuttlebutt talk during those times. The things I remember are things that affected me personally, but others I have apparently pushed back so deep into the archives of my memory bank, where I simply cannot recapture them.

One reason I think my siblings can remember and I cannot is due to the fact I left town when I was still a teen and simply left many of the old things behind—out of sight, out of mind, as some would say. I also believe I have blotted out a lot of bad experiences that were probably jarring to my psyche but retained a few. Another reason may be that by my leaving town so long ago and leaving behind the old, I possibly replaced them with new memories from my travels throughout the Northern Hemisphere over the years, including college and my military experiences. All of my siblings, except one, who grew up and still live in St. Louis have the continuity of growth with those with whom they grew up as well as the places they may still frequent. Also, the things they still do constantly link them with the past. Frankly, I have been out of touch, more than forty years, with childhood friends and contacts I might have had back in the day. My sisters and brothers have maintained most of those contacts and friendships throughout the years while living in the same town. I'm not speaking in terms of the good or bad but simply trying to provide a backdrop to why I cannot remember many events that took place during my childhood, and it sometimes bothers me a little, though not a lot. All of my siblings have retired and are now leading different lives outside of work. My experiences today are very different from theirs, but I have always maintained an unmistakable and unbreakable love for my parents, sisters, and brothers. That in itself gives me much satisfaction and peace of mind because I believe they feel the same.

## Smoke Rising in Pieces

One of the most regretful and challenging fragments of my life was when I began to smoke cigarettes, with an inability to quit. Unlike many young people who picked up a cigarette for the first time, I was not pressured by my peer group, influenced by societal norms, or attracted through advertisements. I picked up my first cigarette when I was eighteen years old, and I have deep regrets that I did. It wasn't because I thought it was cool to smoke or that friends were doing it but, ironically, I began while babysitting my oldest sister, Jimmie's kids. I discovered a pack of cigarettes in a top drawer located in her bedroom. My initial instincts were to leave them alone, but my curiosity got the best of me, and I smoked my first cigarette. My sister's kids were very young. To avoid exposing them to the residual smoke, I found a secure place near a window where I could blow the smoke out without them knowing or leaving the scent of smoke. The first few puff s of smoke made me lightheaded, but that didn't stop me. My sister was not aware of my mischief and each time I looked out for her kids, I would look for her cigarettes and smoke one or two.

I had very few friends who smoked, but over time, I

began to purchase my own pack of cigarettes. This, of course, was the beginning of a long, tough journey of smoking cigarettes, upon which I became addicted. Many years passed without giving much thought to quitting, especially when I began to hang around others who smoked.

It was not until I reached my early twenties that I began to agonize over the prospects of quitting. I had reached this point in my life when I decided to recommit my life to the faith I once had and to Christian living. I had always been taught smoking was a sin and I could not be a Christian if I did. This was certainly a dilemma for Michael J. Washington me because, on the one hand, I enjoyed smoking, and on the other hand, I wanted to live like I thought a Christian should live. I believed if I continued to smoke I couldn't possibly call myself a Christian; it would be hypocritical. I struggled with the fact that I really wanted to quit but found it very difficult, even after praying for God to take the desire away.

During this period, I was so intent on keeping my smoking habit a secret that years passed before my wife and kids even had an inkling that I smoked. I snuck around, only smoking outside our home, and would camouflage the smell through cologne or gum. As they say, sooner or later the truth will find you out, and it did. I was not aware of how addictive cigarettes were until my first attempts to quit. I tried most of the suggested avenues to quit, such as nicotine gum, patches, and prescription medicine. Sometimes I was able to quit, albeit briefly because I would pick the habit up again. I tried to quit cold turkey, and that didn't work for me. I tried reducing the amount of cigarettes I would normally consume on a daily basis, which only lasted for a short while. At one point, I would bum cigarettes, imposing on others through supplication, to avoid buying a pack. However, just short of hypnosis, which I hear has a high success rate, I failed multiple times. Second to drugs, it has been, without a doubt, the biggest prolonged impediment to my physical health and my rational thinking.

To say the least, my cigarette smoking tormented me for many years. I had, for many years, hidden this fact from others and refused to openly admit I smoked, especially within some circles of acquaintances. Therefore, it is with trepidation that I disclose the abhorrence of my past addiction to cigarettes because many who know me were not aware of my habit. Even though I smoked less than a pack a day and knew many chain smokers who smoked two packs a day or more, I rationalized that I was in a different category of smokers. Although ashamed of this habit, I mistakenly believed my health was less compromised and it would be easier for me to quit. Over time, I realized my assessment was simply wrong. My health was jeopardized just as much as the heavier smoker, and many of them seemed to have found it easier to quit cold turkey.

For many years, I felt like a pariah while in the company of those who never smoked cigarettes and who possibly did not understand how hard it is to stop. I had always feared, if exposed, people would view me differently, or I would be cruelly judged, especially by those in the Christian community. They can sometimes be the most critical in judgment. Smoking has also dulled my sense of smell, and I'm acutely aware that the smell of smoke lingers in the clothes I wear, in the car I drive, and in my home when I smoke. I am certainly not proud of this habit and quite frankly frustrated at the fact I continued to smoke even though I knew tobacco can and has caused lung cancer as well as lung and heart diseases.

It is noteworthy to mention a relatively small but important part of my not wanting others to know I smoked is because of the stigma associated with smoking. I can remember days past when smoking was not so much frowned upon and even considered cool. However, nowadays, it appears to be a stain on one's character if he or she smokes. To be perfectly honest, I believe society's prevalent disapproval of smoking is good because lives are in the balance, and I, for one, cannot lament this societal change. Although being forced to smoke outside in the cold, rain, and sometimes-scorching heat made me a little agitated, I adjusted.

I had to also face the fact that part of the reason I hid my smoking addiction was based on pride, which got in the way of my being transparent with the habit. I have witnessed many who have quit smoking and are now enjoying the comforts of their self-restraint. Many of them who managed to overcome the addiction seemed to gain a considerable amount of weight, which is a distressing thought. I have also witnessed some who developed serious health complications from smoking but still continued, which is even more troubling. This, I believe, is a testament to how difficult it is to quit.

This particular addiction is so strong that even when I had the flu or a cold, and it made me cough and left an awful taste in my throat, I was still unable to resist putting a cigarette to my lips. On these occasions when the taste of cigarette smoking was at its worst, I was constantly reminded of the addictive components of the nicotine, which has both physical and psychological ramifications. The physical aspect of this dichotomy is that I increasingly became irritable from the withdrawals of the nicotine through the incessant habit I acquired through the passage of time.

As I consider all of the negative effects of smoking, I also acknowledge the compelling reasons why I continued. I enjoyed it after a good meal, and when I occasionally had a drink, it seemed to relieve minor stresses I may have had at a given moment. After smoking for many years and at that critical junction of my life, I came to a very sobering thought I had to confront. Besides the addiction, my primary reason for not quitting was the fact that my will to quit was not as strong as my desire to continue and, in my case, could not happen without some kind of external assistance. Those who never smoked before probably would not have a clue how difficult it was to quit, and some might even be quick to pass moral judgment, which I had to accept. I accepted the fact that smoking cigarettes was harmful to my physical health and I might not quit. I have also determined that smoking did not prevent me from being a child of God but was a spiritual Achilles' heel in my life. I realize many would disagree with this determination, but I believe my final arbiter and judgment will come from God, not man, which gives me peace. However, my final words on this matter are that choosing not to use tobacco is probably one of the best things one can do for his health. Don't smoke!

# CHAPTER 15

## The Ultimate Guardian of My Peace

Securing consistent peace in your life is not guaranteed. Neither is it a destination. I see it as a journey's call to augment the precious passage of time. The safeguard of my securing peace within my subconscious thoughts is defined and cemented by a fundamental Christian biblical perspective. My peace comes from my knowledge and trust in God, which stems from my early childhood. My exposure to the concept of God and Christianity was conceived at an early stage in my life. When my siblings and I were very young, my mother took us to church every Sunday. We attended the Church of God in Christ, a denomination of the Pentecostal persuasion. This denomination is very lively and one that breeds a particular practice of worship just as many other religions do. Without getting into the specifics of the Pentecostal doctrine, I was strongly influenced by its teachings and practices, which were the impetus of my initial desire to become a Christian. The beginning of my desire to serve Christ was my first experience during a church service, when I was about ten years old, an experience I will never forget. It was during the early part of the worship service where there was singing, praising, and shouting, all demonstrating a form of worship to God. I was sitting on a pew singing and sincerely enjoying the service when, all of a sudden, an overpowering presence came upon me from nowhere that I could tell. It is not easy to explain, but I began to feel a tremendous force of energy move from the top of my head reverberating down through the rest of my body to my feet. It was as fast as a lightning bolt striking an inanimate object, bringing it to life, and powerful as an electrical force but gentle as a smooth breeze to my countenance. It was the best feeling I have ever experienced in my life. It made me move, it made me jump, and it made me shout, none of which I had done or had the inkling to do before. From that day forward, I believe, my life began to take a new trajectory, because I began to think differently, act differently, and see things differently. I had only a limited understanding of who God is, how I could be saved, and how to walk in His way.

Shortly afterwards, I was baptized in water, the first time in my life, which preceded a full confession of my sins and a conviction to do the best I could to follow the tenets of Christian living. I was conscious of everything I said and did and conducted my daily affairs relative to the faith I had acquired at that tender age. I felt different and estranged from most others within my age bracket because I wanted to live the way I had been taught, in light of biblical teaching. Most of my friends had not been exposed to those teachings or, if they had, decided not to live in that way. At that age, my view of the church and Christian living was fresh and newly conceived, sprinkled with a taste of exceptionalism and excitement.

## Abiding Spirit Within

As I grew older into my early teens, while enmeshed in a sea of nonbelievers, I began to fall prey to peer pressure and did things contrary to my newfound beliefs and teachings. Although my thoughts and motives remained pure, I seemed compelled to follow the crowd and experiment with certain acts of immorality, violating the moral principles I had confessed to adhere to. I stopped attending church around the age of thirteen, after which I found myself moving down the slippery slope of incredulity that served no rhyme or reason. I had subjected myself to certain behaviors that replicated what others did, such as lying, cheating, and stealing. But I never seemed to succeed without being called out or caught. By the time I reached the age of fifteen, I had obviously strayed from my moral compass and suspended my growth in Christ. Ironically, while only in my teens, certain family members would call me preacher, but I'm not sure why because I never had the interest or aspiration to become one.

As a young man in my twenties and thirties, I wandered in the wilderness of self-indulgence trying to have a dexterous life of immorality while professing to know God and constantly enduring the pieces of life. Even then I managed to maintain a peaceful countenance, which I never understood until later in life. I sincerely believe my peace is fundamentally and wholly contributable to my way of thinking, concealed by my overall attitude toward life and, more importantly, cloaked with the love I have for others. The knowledge and presence of God in my life has been and continues to be the most powerful influence in my life.

## Belief Systems

Many of our belief systems play a role toward living a peaceful life. My exposure to Christ at an early age provided my belief system. All of us have a belief system, whether we believe in the prominently known teachings of Catholicism, Protestantism, Buddhism, Mormonism, Confucianism, Hinduism, agnosticism, or Islam. Even if you are an atheist, you have a belief system. What we believe shapes who we are and informs our every action. The underlying premise of what we believe, for the most part, is derived from whether or not God exists. Whether we choose to believe in God or not is a choice and does not preclude the fact that we all have a belief system. We may not consciously think about it, but our values and beliefs drive the very rudiments of our conduct and behavior. Therefore, it stands to reason that the beliefs we hold are predicated upon whether or not we believe there is a God. Either we do or we do not. I believe one's belief system is an incontrovertible yet prevailing, oxymoronic nature and concept that captures the underlying pretentious state of mind in all human beings. I believe it is without a doubt that our belief systems play crucial role in the way we conduct daily affairs and ultimately informs our ideas about human compassion, aggression, and submission. What we believe is essentially the guiding force behind the choices we make, right or wrong, good or bad. The intriguing by-product of what we believe is the incongruous nature or inconstant disposition we possess throughout our life's experience. Both are incorporated through a profound sense of being that dominates the human experience.

Our belief system also captures a deep way of thinking whether it is embraced through morality or spirituality. There is a difference. Most of us have a strong sense of morality, but few possess the essential component of spirituality, which is appropriated through the gift of God's Holy Spirit. The substance of spirituality stems from the essence of one's religious belief and conviction in God. It is sacred and comes from within. On the other hand, morality is the art of separating or differentiating right from wrong or making the distinction between good and bad, primarily based on a conformity to rules of the appropriate conduct or behavior within a given culture. Being moral can give a sense of purpose and lead you to feel better about yourself. The opposite is true when submitting to the Holy Spirit, which can actually help uproot pride, arrogance, and superiority. The true difference between morality and spirituality is that morality is contrived and controlled by your primal desire to be good, which conforms to society's norms. Spirituality is driven by its essence of God's spirit within, which is love, patience, kindness, gentleness, and peace. Therefore, it is easy to conclude that you can be moral without being spiritual. However, if you are abiding by God's spirit, morality is a by-product. A moral conscience will also dictate what others should or shouldn't do, but the indwelling of God's spirit will direct certain things you will or will not do.

In other words, if you truly believe in God and believe he has given you his Holy Spirit, His spirit can be a guide to carry out His will in your life. His spirit within you will not force you to do anything, but if you allow it to influence your life, it will direct your steps and give you peace. It is not anyone's place to impose his or her will onto anyone because God has given all of us the ability to choose his way or another. When I hear people talk about their spiritual convictions while seemingly imposing their views onto others, I wonder if they truly understand what it means to have a spiritual conviction. I believe no one's religious or spiritual conviction should infringe on what others believe or what they practice. It is certainly true that a spiritual conviction of someone is real, sacred, and needs to be respected, but it is just as true that others will hold similar convictions reserved to direct their own habits and behavior. It is without doubt your convictions should be made known to advance the word of God, but a true spiritual conviction of faith is not for a believer to force others to conform or provoke others who do not agree. It should, instead, be reserved to direct a personal spiritual walk in life. This is simply my personal opinion and my spiritual conviction of my faith, which bears witness to a desire for clarity of judgment.

My belief system and values were developed at an early age when I was first able to conceptualize the difference between right and wrong. I have carried this belief system over the past six decades. Although my beliefs in the variations and dimensions of Christianity have evolved during my life's journey, I have not wavered from a primary belief in Jesus Christ, whom I believe is the only way to salvation. This fundamental belief has guided my steps toward salvation and will never change. It is the essential ingredient for my peaceful walk, despite the troubled pieces in my life. The pieces include the many mistakes due to my own human flaws, shortcomings, and poor choices.

While growing up, I didn't understand or realize I had the spirit of Christ within me patiently waiting to be given control.

By the time I reached my early twenties, I had experienced and witnessed a lot of turmoil in the lives of others. I had seen much corruption from those who possessed power and influence over others. I had seen unnecessary divisions among family and friends. I had seen people using all kinds of deceptive practices to promote themselves, and I had seen friends and foe alike misuse, mistreat, and mislead each other, causing confusion and disorder in relationships. As I reflected on these things, I didn't want any part of them. I knew they were contrary to God's way and could only yield destruction.

When I was twenty-two years old, I began to feel like a fish out of water and felt a burden to change my circumstances, which meant turning my life around and returning to the faith I once had when I was only a child. This revelation led me to finding a place to worship God and to be in the midst of like minds. I began attending a church in Harlem, New York, where I recommitted my faith and was baptized in water for the second time. Unlike the Pentecostal church where I grew up, this church professed a prominent aspect of the apostolic faith, but both incorporated the same denominational brand. I was in my early twenties and possessed the maturity I didn't have when I first accepted Christ in my life. But I was still immature in many ways, because I had not truly grasped the essence of the Christian walk. After five years attending, I had grown spiritually and was ordained deacon when I was twenty-seven. The church was relatively small, with a congregation of about three hundred devoted Christians whom I enjoyed and appreciated the fellowship of over the years. I knew the pastor, his son, and son-in-law very well because we golfed together frequently. At one point, I considered working for the church in a maintenance capacity, but wisdom dictated the job was not for me. As I matured mentally and spiritually, I began to see things that appeared to be contrary to God's word, and I became slightly disenchanted with the idea of staying at this church. My wife attended the church as well. She grew up in the church, was baptized in the church, and we were married in the church. She saw things a little differently than I; thus, I did not want to bring division between the two of us, and I remained in the church until we both were of like minds.

Over time, my wife and I felt the same and decided to leave the church. Since we were well respected and considered pillars of the church, the pastor told the entire congregation they could not speak or have anything to do with us, including my wife's father, brother, sister, and my best friend who attended the church. We were not surprised by this unthinkable declaration because parishioners had left before we did, and he gave similar declarations. His threat to the congregation was simple; they would be dis-fellowshipped or removed if word got back they had violated his proclamation. This was a sad affair because many of our friends followed his edict, and communication between us discontinued. For many years, my wife's father, brother, and sister and my best friend didn't speak to us. Years later, the silence changed slightly. Many others have seen the light and left this church over time. Obviously, this kind of strict adherence was not in God's word but a man-made concept in order to control God's flock of people. I was thirty years old when I left that church. I had no regrets because I knew a building with walls was not the church but that God's people are.

## Another Church and Doctrinal Change

We left the church in the early eighties. My peace of mind was never affected by leaving this church. We began attending and worshipping at a different church with a different doctrine. I considered this to be a new beginning of my Christian walk. The church teachings and practices were very new for me, especially after having initially been exposed to Pentecostal teachings. After becoming familiar with their teachings, we moved to Wisconsin in 1983 for about fifteen months, where I attended Wisconsin University. Within some circles, this church was considered a cult because of its legalistic and somewhat unorthodox doctrines. Of course, I did not see it quite that way and began to take becoming a member seriously. I guess I was impressed by its unique teachings while, at the time, the church was reaching its membership's peak of about 145,000.

Although I had previously been baptized, I was baptized again and became an official member while in Wisconsin. I began to observe the many laws from the Old Testament, some of which included not partaking of unclean meats, observing annual festivals, and the strict adherence to keeping and worshipping on the Sabbath. It was a challenge for me personally to give up some meats claimed to be biblically unclean for consumption, but I managed to follow those practices. As I recall, prior to my becoming a member, a Jewish coworker who observed the Sabbath could not work during those hours, which infringed upon her beliefs. When she was placed on shifts that were in conflict with her faith, she would ask me to trade my shift for hers, and I would gladly do so. There were, at times, little scuttlebutt talks around the office concerning her beliefs, but I would always take her side, not realizing one day would come when I would be in the same situation as she, having to trade my shifts because of my religious beliefs and convictions. A few years later, I was removed from this somewhat awkward predicament when I was promoted and transferred to work a day job.

One of the most fulfilling obligational practices while with the church was attending the annual feasts. Through these practices, my family and I were afforded the opportunity to travel throughout the country and sometimes abroad to observe annual festivals. These were a few highlights with this church while serving God in my own innocent way. I say this in hindsight, because I believe it was spiritual digression for me. I had strayed from the traditional fundamental teachings of the word of God, which clearly states we are not bound by the laws of the Old Testament but are saved by grace and not through works. After saying that, I believe my experience with the church was not in vain; again, my peace of mind was never affected. I served in many capacities, such as deacon, youth leader, usher board director, and president of both the spokesman and graduate clubs, all of which contributed to my spiritual growth and maturation. Although I had been ordained before, becoming deacon was not a position I pursued because of the tremendous responsibilities it demanded, even though the work I did leading to it was befitting. Being a youth leader allowed me to guide and mentor young people. Having been appointed usher board director allowed me to develop leadership skills by supervising many adults from various backgrounds and professions. The spokesman clubs were like a training ground for public speaking and helped me to deliver a speech in or out of church without trepidation.

## Faith and Deliverance

In the early 1990s, my family and I moved from New York City to Charleston, West Virginia. Prior to leaving New York, rumors were afoot claiming the church would be issuing a new statement of faith, accepting traditional Bible doctrine in many areas. The potential doctrinal changes posed no issue for me because I was already familiar with many traditional biblical teachings. Moving to West Virginia was a huge contrast to New York City, in that the pace was much slower. The church I attended was small and encompassed an older congregation with many spiritual and devout Christians who made me feel at home. With this church, small cell groups were formed to promulgate and reinforce God's word using intimate settings. I presided over a small cell group that met at my home once a week.

After a couple of years with the church, I became very close to many of its parishioners. As stated earlier, the church was a small congregation of mature spiritual-minded believers.

The pastor, elders, and deacons would meet once a week for prayer and spiritual growth. I recall my mother had been ill with breast cancer but still managed to come to West Virginia for a visit. I took her to this church, and these same devout Christian folk prayed for her as well. The cancer went into remission and has not returned. Many members of the church kept in contact with her for several years after she left. It has been nearly twenty years since then, but my mother still talks about those caring Christians in West Virginia. They really had a powerful impact on her, and she is forever grateful for their love, genuine concern, and outreach to her. My experience with these church members will forever be in my heart because of their genuine nature and spiritual maturity.

## Moving Forward with Change

In the late nineties, we moved to the Washington, DC, metro area. I remained a member of the same church. By this time, changes in the church's doctrine began to cause the church to splinter into several smaller churches. Some completely separated, forming a new church altogether. Eventually, the church I attended parted and became a self-identified church of its own. This allowed the church to function and worship as a complete and separate entity. The new church provided its own spiritual guidance for about 150 churchgoers. I personally welcomed the change and was fully committed to these biblical principles and teachings, which I had accepted early in my childhood.

I was a member of this particular church for about twelve years but left to begin worshiping along with other mature Christians in home group settings who felt the need to separate from the routine cadence of common church worship. As with many within the Christian community, this group of Christians believes the truest form of one's Christian walk is having a personal relationship with Christ. They also believe that worshiping Christ is a daily walk by utilizing his Holy Spirit to guide behaviors. Leaving the church was not easy but a decision I felt convicted to do. I still have the same respect and reverence for those Christians, and I love them no less than before I left. I also continue to believe these Christians are true children of God and we all are simply moving toward the same goal but have a slightly different way of serving him. May God bless and prosper this devout group of Christians who love unconditionally and who trust, as I do, that Christ is coming soon.

For most of my adult life, I have attempted to live for Christ, not in a perfect way but in one that honors and trusts God's word that he will make a way for me to live with his dignity and, through his saving grace, provide me the salvation I so desperately need. We live in a deceitful world filled with evil, malevolence, and malicious malcontent. As with many facets of life, I believe Christians will also live in pieces, experiencing adversities, sufferings, and hardships.

But we have a hope, and that hope is in Christ Jesus, who shed his blood and died for all mankind. But Jesus was resurrected, and his spirit now lives within us. This life is short, but all Christians who accept Christ as Lord and savior have the faith that he lives and the confidence of eternal life. Despite my sometimes-aberrant ways, I believe, without a doubt, Christ is the ultimate guardian of my peace.

# CHAPTER 16
• • • • • • • • • • •
## Anchored in Peace

To enjoy a consistently peaceful life does not mean you will not encounter problems, disappointments, or difficulties, which are essentially forms of peace intruders. Many problems we face are within our control to solve, but indeed some are not. However, I sincerely believe anyone can absolutely overcome the many obstacles faced in a lifetime. Unfortunately, many still find it difficult or impossible to get beyond the resulting hurt, scars, and pain we encounter. In summary, living in peace requires the ability to be calm, conciliatory, gentle, patient, undisturbed, or unruffled even when there is the opposite with conflict, discord, disruption, or confusion. It requires being calm during turbulent times, conciliatory to gain good will or favor, patient when there is obvious conflict, undisturbed even when there is discord, and gentle when there is violence. These associated temperaments may be a little difficult to manage but can become natural with practice. Life's journey can be short, fragmented, turbulent, and glazed with stress but can definitely be balanced with contentment, dependent upon your outlook on life.

## Lessons Learned Embodied with Success

Now that I'm a mature adult, I can look back at my past and truly confirm I have been blessed to have a peaceful covering on my life even while living and encountering many pieces. Through many lessons, I've learned many things that gave me the wherewithal to be the best person I could be. I learned to love people the way I want to be loved. I learned to embrace patience because there were many times when I needed others to be patient with me. I learned to make sacrifices for others who would benefit more than I. I learned pride is a huge character flaw and breeds discontentment, and that fear is a state of mind that is protective but can disable rational thought. I learned not to take things personally even though people will always say negative things about me, because their words are hollow and meaningless unless I give them power. I learned to forgive because forgiving frees my mind from internal strife. And lastly, I learned passing judgment onto others is easy, but judging myself is a more profitable assessment. These lessons learned have elevated my ability to be a better person and increased my ability to embody unconditional love, enabling me to walk in peace.

Looking back at all of my life's trials and accomplishments, I can see clearly how I have maintained peace in my life and what I believe to be the true essence of success. According to customary standards, success is generally regarded in terms of the attainment of wealth or position. Many view success as having gained a certain amount of financial stability. Others view success as acquiring a position of power where they have control and authority over others. Some conventionally view success as having great power and influence on people and events. And yet others may view success as having many undisputable friends over a lifetime. Although all of these seemingly certitudes suggest having been successful in some form or fashion, they cannot guarantee peace. If all of these were valid to sustain success in life, they would absolutely be able to bear the rigorous, pernicious battle scars life has to offer, but none of them can. In my view, success is living with a very high peace quotient where peace and success coexist. All of us have the potential to be successful, but many fail this test of time. I believe real success has longevity and is sustainable. This premise is my own conceptual view of the power in peaceful living and is based on my life's experiences. When you have peace, you involuntary accomplish being successful. It is not something you work toward but is simply a by-product of peace. Throughout my entire life, I have lived in pieces but have literally lived in peace. This sounds like a contradiction but is a profound concept and one I have considered thoughtfully.

## Subjective Discourse of My Peace

My early childhood set the stage for my life's journey. Each step I took to reach adulthood was influenced by my childhood experiences. I was a normal child raised by imperfect parents. I grew up in an imperfect family and functioned in an imperfect environment. I conducted my affairs in an imperfect society while being encompassed by an imperfect world. All of these imperfections had direct and residual effects on my growth and maturation toward adulthood. From the time I was a young boy, I was careful of how I treated people—family, friends, and foes alike. I was taught to treat others like I wanted to be treated, to be respectful to others, to give people the benefit of the doubt, and most importantly, to be honest to myself. These were instilled in me as a child, and during my maturation toward adulthood, I always tried to live up to those standards. The way I have internalized my environment may be different from how others have, but all of us must confront the unexpected. The lens (senses) from which I view my surroundings is also a common attribute. The trials of life—dealing with failures, disappointments, temptations, grief, and pain—are the same for everyone.

As I glance back at the pieces of my life and my journey, the way I control my emotions seems to play a significant role in my being able to have peace. Many of our actions emanate from the way we think and feel. Therefore, I believe we must, at all times, make sure our emotional responses to life's challenges are tamed with patience and with rational thought. Even though

I continue to be confronted with disappointments, difficulties, and stresses, I am at a stage in my life where I truly know who I am and realize an undeniable certainty, which is that my life has been and continues to be anchored in peace.

www.ingramcontent.com/pod-product-compliance
Lightning Source LLC
Chambersburg PA
CBHW072054110526
44590CB00018B/3168